RICHARD P. CINCOTTA · ROBERT ENGELMAN · DANIELE ANASTASION

THE SECURITY DEMOGRAPHIC

POPULATION AND CIVIL CONFLICT AFTER THE COLD WAR

POPULATION ACTION INTERNATIONAL

© 2003 Population Action International

1300 19th Street NW, Second Floor
Washington, DC 20036
USA

Telephone: [+1] 202.557.3400   Fax: [+1] 202.728.4177
www.populationaction.org

For copies of this publication, please send an e-mail request to pubinq@popact.org

Population Action
I N T E R N A T I O N A L

Publications Production Manager: Brian Hewitt
Editor: Mimi Harrison
Research Assistants: Jennifer Kaczor, Ellen Davis, Eric Steiner, Jennifer Dusenberry, Akia Talbot

Design and production: Meadows Design Office, Inc., Washington, DC, www.mdomedia.com
Creative director and designer: Marc Alain Meadows
Assistant graphic designer: Nancy Bratton

Cover photo © Sven Torfinn/ Panos Pictures. Ivory Coast, Bouake, October 2002.

Printing: Schmitz Press, Sparks, MD. This publication was printed with soy-based inks on elementally
chlorine-free paper composed of 50 percent recycled content with 35 percent post-cosumer waste. ⊕ ♲ ♨

ISBN: 1-889735-48-5
Library of Congress Control Number: 2003113669

Printed in the United States of America
07 06   05   04   03   5   4   3   2   1

THE SECURITY DEMOGRAPHIC

A DECADE OF RISK, 2000–10:
A GLOBAL ASSESSMENT OF THE DEMOGRAPHIC RISK OF CIVIL CONFLICT

About half of the world's countries exhibit demographic characteristics that add to their risk of a civil conflict during the current decade. This assessment of demographic risk from 2000 to 2010 is based on the intensity of three stress factors: the proportion of those aged 15 to 29 in the adult population, the rate of urban population growth, and the per capita availability of cropland and fresh water. Because this demographic analysis is based solely on national data, it does not reflect high intensities of these demographic factors at the sub-national level, an important consideration in geographically large countries, including Brazil, China, India, Indonesia and Russia. The nine countries indicated with an extremely high rate of working-age adult death (losing 10 percent or more of the 15-to-64-year-old population in five years), largely reflecting the influence of the HIV/AIDS pandemic, are Botswana, Central African Republic, Lesotho, Malawi, Mozambique, Namibia, Swaziland, Zambia, and Zimbabwe. Another 14 countries (not indicated on the map) are experiencing the death of 7 to 10 percent of their working-age population every 5 years.

LEVEL OF DEMOGRAPHIC RISK

VERY HIGH RISK   EXTREMELY HIGH RATE OF DEATH AMONG WORKING-AGE ADULTS

HIGH RISK

ELEVATED RISK

OTHER COUNTRIES

NO DATA

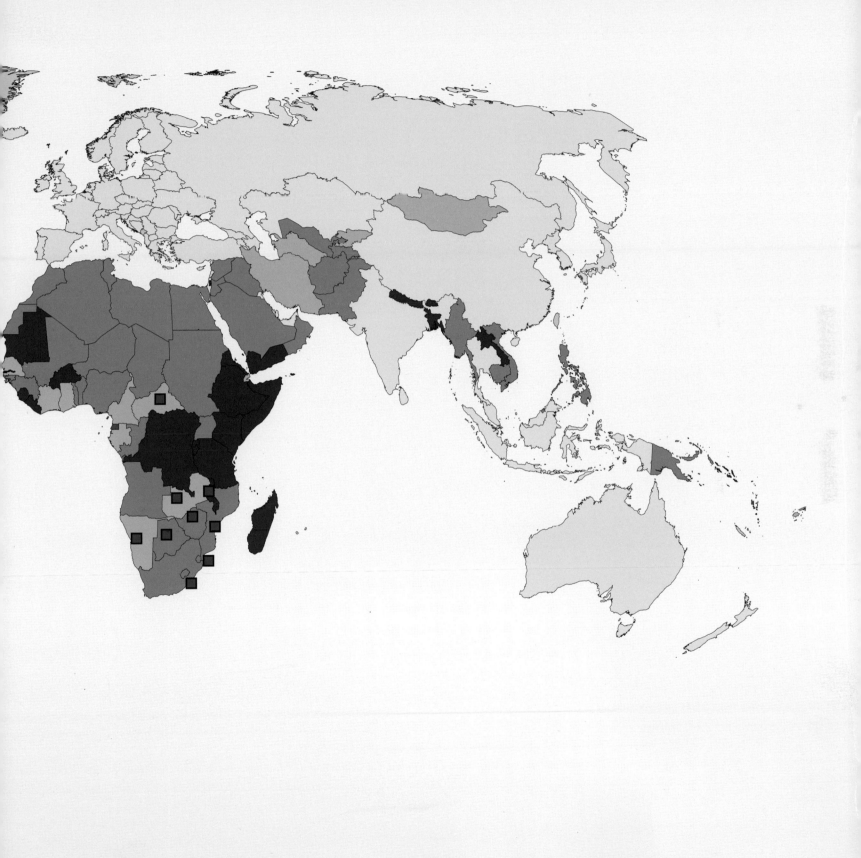

TO WILLIAM H. DRAPER, JR.

August 10, 1894 – December 26, 1974

The authors dedicate this report to the memory of Major General William H. Draper, Jr., a founder in 1965 and later chair of the Population Crisis Committee (now Population Action International). Following retirement from the U.S. Army, Gen. Draper served as Undersecretary of the Army during the Truman Administration and played key roles in the post-World War II reconstruction of Europe and Japan, led by U.S. Secretary of State (and retired General of the Army) George C. Marshall. In 1952–53, William Draper served with the rank of ambassador as United States Special Representative in Europe. Asked by President Eisenhower in 1958 to lead a commission studying U.S. military assistance, he became convinced of the strategic necessity of addressing long-term population growth, and spent the remainder of his life persuading a succession of U.S. presidents and Congress to support the global expansion of voluntary family planning services. A major fundraiser for the International Planned Parenthood Foundation, Gen. Draper later secured U.S. government support for the establishment of the United Nations Fund for Population Activities (UNFPA, later renamed the United Nations Population Fund). He is credited with the idea of making the UN World Conference on Population, held in Bucharest in 1974, a meeting of governments aimed at shaping global policy, rather than one in which demographers and other experts simply discussed population. The Bucharest conference led eventually to the historic International Conference on Population and Development in Cairo in 1994 and its Programme of Action, agreed to by 179 governments, a lasting legacy for William Draper's lifetime of service.

CONTENTS

ILLUSTRATIONS

ACKNOWLEDGMENTS

The authors thank the following individuals for their help in locating data or literature for the report, or for otherwise providing guidance in this effort: Thomas Buettner, Ellen Brennan-Galvin, Anne Gujon, Craig Lasher, Christian Mesquida, Shaheen Mohadar, Keith Montgomery, Naohiro Ogawa, Scott Radloff, Robert Retherford, Robert P. Richardson, Henrik Urdal, and Hania Zlotnik. We also acknowledge the following individuals who, often in addition to other assistance, provided valuable review and editorial assistance: Kenneth Bacon, Terri Bartlett, Nelle Temple Brown, Beth Chaleki, Barbara Crane, Amy Coen, Geoffrey Dabelko, Roger-Mark De Souza, Sally Ethelston, Mimi Harrison, Allen Hecht, Thomas Hooper, Leslie Johnston, Stuart Kingma, Jennifer Kaczor, Kimberley Cline, Robert Lalasz, Jonathan Lash, Tom Outlaw, Barbara Seligman, John Sewell, and Rodger Yeager. The authors extend a special thanks to the Environmental Change and Security Project and its parent institution, the Woodrow Wilson Center for International Scholars, for hosting an oral review of an early draft.

SUMMARY

Do the dynamics of human population—rates of growth, age structure, distribution and more—influence when and where warfare will next break out? The findings of this report suggest that the risks of *civil conflict* (deadly violence between governments and non-state insurgents, or between state factions within territorial boundaries) that are generated by demographic factors may be much more significant than generally recognized, and worthy of more serious consideration by national security policymakers and researchers. Its conclusions—drawn from a review of literature and analyses of data from 180 countries, about half of which experienced civil conflict at some time from 1970 through 2000—argue that:

Recent progress along the *demographic transition*—a population's shift from high to low rates of birth and death—is associated with continuous declines in the vulnerability of nation-states to civil conflict. If this association continues through the 21st century, then a range of policies promoting small, healthy and better educated families and long lives among populations in developing countries seems likely to encourage greater political stability in weak states and to enhance global security in the future.

Key Findings

The research results presented in this report [for more summarized detail see the briefing points at the end of each chapter] lead to seven key findings:

- During the 1970s, '80s and '90s, countries in the late phases of demographic transition were less likely to experience outbreaks of civil conflicts than those still in the transition's early or middle phases. And, more crucially, that likelihood decreased for high-risk countries as they experienced overall declines in birth and death rates, and thus entered the later phases of demographic transition. On average, the decline in the annual birth rate of five births per thousand people corresponded to a decline of about 5 percent in the likelihood of civil conflict during the following decade—descending from more than 40 percent likelihood in the earliest phase of demographic transition to less than 5 percent in the latest. While this association does not suggest direct causation, the relationships found here are striking and consistent.

- Demographic processes neither lead inevitably to, nor do they eliminate the risk of, civil conflict. Several demographically high-risk states may have offset some risk by facilitating emigration and encouraging remittances (savings sent home by emigrant workers), distributing farmland, creating urban employment, addressing ethnic grievances, or alternatively, by ruthlessly repressing dissent. In a few countries where progress along the demographic transition should have helped alleviate risk—such as Colombia, Northern Ireland (United Kingdom) and Sri Lanka—costly civil conflicts that first emerged in earlier decades continued to be waged (although in Northern Ireland and Sri Lanka this may be changing).

■ The demographic factors most closely associated with the likelihood of an outbreak of civil conflict during the 1990s were a high proportion of young adults (aged 15 to 29 years)—a phenomenon referred to as a *youth bulge*—and a rapid rate of urban population growth. Countries in which young adults comprised more than 40 percent of the adult population were more than twice as likely as countries with lower proportions to experience an outbreak of civil conflict. States with urban population growth rates above 4 percent were about twice as likely to sustain the outbreak of a civil conflict as countries with lower rates.

■ Countries with low-availability categories of cropland and/or renewable fresh water, measured on a per capita basis, were 1.5 times as likely to experience civil conflict as those in other categories. While water scarcity has gained attention in the past as a likely predisposing condition for interstate war and civil tensions between ethnic regions, land-related threats to traditional rural livelihoods, such as disputes over farmland distribution or settlement of outsiders into traditional ethnic homelands, have featured more prominently in the evolution of recent civil conflicts than tensions over water.

■ Currently available data cannot verify that a high death rate among working-age adults, a characteristic of populations with high HIV prevalence, contributes to a state's vulnerability to civil conflict. Nonetheless, the arguments for the connection—citing the loss of key professionals, the weakening of military units, and the unprecedented numbers of orphans—are strong, and the projected demographic impact of HIV/AIDS is likely to exceed by far that of the 1980s and 1990s.

■ Demographic factors do not act alone in producing stresses that can challenge government leadership and the functional capacity of states. Key demographic characteristics that increase the risk of civil conflict interact with each other and with non-demographic factors, such as historic ethnic tensions, unresponsive governance and ineffective institutions. This compounds the net risk for countries in the early or middle phases of demographic transition.

■ For the near future, the highest demographic risks of civil conflict are concentrated in sub-Saharan Africa, in the Middle East and in South Asia. An exercise of identifying countries with multiple risk factors, based on projected population data from 2000 to 2005, identifies 25 mostly African and Asian countries that have reached critical levels in the three principal demographic stress factors considered in this report (high proportion of youth, rapid urban growth, and exceptionally low levels of cropland and/or fresh water per person). Ten countries that had reached critical levels in these three factors also are experiencing excessive adult mortality, mostly due to high HIV prevalence—an additional factor likely to exacerbate risk levels for civil conflict that are already dangerously high.

The Security Demographic

Both the results of our analyses and a robust literature on demographic change and security support the central—and hopeful—conclusion of this report: Progress through the demographic transition helps reduce the risk of civil conflict, and thus contributes to a more peaceful and secure world. Over the past 40 years this progress has been impressive, albeit uneven, in all of the world's regions.

Human population worldwide is growing at nearly half the pace of 35 years ago, and infant mortality and family size are roughly half what they were. Most countries are moving toward what we call here a *security demographic,* a distinctive range of population structures and dynamics that make civil conflict less likely. Movement in this direction, however, is uneven and in peril. Continuing declines in birthrates and increases in life expectancy in the poorest and worst-governed countries will require much more international collaboration and assistance than are evident today, and greater efforts to improve the lives of women and increase their participation in government and throughout society. These conclusions and the research that supports them lead, in turn, to four broad recommendations, designed specifically for security policymakers and analysts. The recommendations follow this summary.

RECOMMENDATIONS

The policies and programs that influence population trends are properly the sphere of health and social service agencies and organizations, and donors of international assistance. Military, diplomatic and intelligence communities nonetheless can play important roles. Transcending partisanship and election cycles, these groups can provide accurate information and guidance to policymakers on population change and the policies that influence it. There may be opportunities for more direct action as well, especially within peacekeeping missions and in the post-conflict environment. The following recommendations are a starting point in suggesting what those in security-related fields can do to link sound population, health and social policies to a more secure future:

1. Promote demographic transition, the progress of populations from high to low rates of birth and death.

■ Help mobilize political will for services that enable women and couples to choose for themselves the timing and frequency of pregnancy and childbirth, that promote maternal and infant survival, and that protect reproductive-age adults from HIV and other sexually transmitted infections.

■ Support international efforts that lengthen and strengthen girls' education, help improve women's access to income-generating opportunities, and help promote child survival.

■ Articulating for policymakers the relationships between population dynamics and armed conflict can help secure funding for programs in family planning, girls' education, maternal and child health and HIV/AIDS prevention and treatment, which together encourage lower birth and death rates in countries still advancing through the demographic transition.

2. Help make access to reproductive health services easier for refugees, civilians in post-conflict environments, and all military personnel.

■ While offering services to local civilians and refugees is generally beyond the scope of most operations, military commands should be prepared to lend logistical and organizational support to those charged with offering reproductive health care in post-conflict environments. These organizations include the United Nations Population Fund (UNFPA) and the UN High Commissioner for Refugees (UNHCR) in the case of refugees, and non-governmental organizations (NGOs) and government ministries of health for other populations.

■ Encourage governments with exemplary HIV/AIDS prevention and treatment programs in their armed forces to participate in military-to-military and military-to-civilian cooperative activities. Encourage donor governments to allow reproductive health programs to address the problems of military personnel and their families, and increase funding for such cooperation.

■ Support and implement policies that assure that reproductive health care of a high standard—including comprehensive contraceptive information and services, prevention of sexually transmitted diseases, and maternal and child health care—is available to all military personnel under all circumstances. Prioritize HIV prevention among military personnel to reduce prevalence among them and to minimize the risk that they will be a source of further infection.

3. Support improvements in the legal, educational and economic status of women.

■ Improvements in women's status can influence social environments, help change cultural norms, and ultimately speed demographic transition. Where possible, encourage social and political reforms that help girls stay in school, offer women economic opportunities, and reward achievement regardless of gender. Qualified women serving in important and visible diplomatic and military roles also serve as models for changes in attitudes at home and abroad.

■ Encourage women to work in government and seek political office and to participate in conflict prevention and post-conflict negotiations. Their participation could ultimately lead to shifts in priorities favoring human development over continued strife.

■ Promote understanding of and sensitivity to the use of violence against women in post-conflict and refugee settings, and work to prevent and discourage such violence. Aside from the moral argument for such a task, violence against women is an instrument in cultural and ethical frameworks that demean women, restrict their status and power, and thus retard progress through the demographic transition.

4. Make demography part of the analysis.

■ Include demographic data and projections in area studies, operational environment forecasts, and other security and threat assessments. Consider the security implications of trends in age structure, AIDS mortality rates and other demographic factors elaborated in this report.

■ Consider the potential for demographic change and its social and economic implications, and allow for a variety of possible demographic futures — as portrayed, for example, by the United Nations Population Division's low, medium and high projections.

■ Encourage the development of demographic and health expertise throughout the military and intelligence communities, and deploy this expertise to inform foreign policy discussions through official testimony and interactions with policymakers, the news media and opinion leaders.

INTRODUCTION

If war is hell, it is also a momentous demographic event. Deaths of combatants and civilians and flows of refugees can alter the size, age structure and ethnic mix of population for years to come. But can demographic change influence war? In recent decades scholars and intelligence analysts have taken up this question, and some have gathered evidence that certain population trends may indeed affect the risk of conflict.

This publication offers an overview of the research relating demographic characteristics to a particular subset of conflicts: *civil conflicts*—those that occur within nation-states and threaten their governments, the social order, and the rate and path of their development. With many weak states unwilling or unable to eliminate terrorist and other violent non-state organizations or expel these groups from their territory, the dynamics of civil conflicts have powerful regional and global implications. This report examines patterns of civil conflict that have emerged since the end of the Cold War, and it considers a further question about this connection: Could governments strengthen the security of strategic states, pivotal regions and the world as a whole by addressing key factors related to demographic change? Our analysis addresses demographic relationships to conflict principally through a lens known to population specialists as the *demographic transition*—the transformation of a population from short lives and many births to long lives and fewer births—and its associations with civil conflicts that emerged from 1990 through 2000. The principal intended audience is the security community: policymakers and analysts in national defense, diplomatic or intelligence agencies and multilateral organizations charged with a regional or global security role.

Objective

Few publications have comprehensively reviewed and discussed the range of arguments purporting demographic risks of armed conflict, and fewer still have assessed their merits statistically. This report sets out to do just that. It provides security policymakers and analysts with an overview of key demographic trends and a framework for understanding the social, economic, environmental and political challenges these trends engender. The report's analysis then applies this same demographic framework, country by country, to offer insight into the current and near-future global risk environment for civil conflict and related instabilities.

The Foundations of this Research

Studies of the nexus of population and armed conflict rest on a broad foundation. Much of today's research draws upon the demographic insights of Herbert Moller in the late 1960s and the work of Nazli Choucri from the early 1970s to the present.[1] Many U.S. diplomats first encountered these arguments in influential national security reports and foreign policy essays by State Department analysts during the 1970s and 1980s, and through organizations advocating that the United States increase foreign assistance spending for family planning programs overseas.[2] Despite this work, the immediacy of Cold War tensions kept population issues at the margins of security concerns.

That changed with the decline in Soviet power. A spate of unexpected post-Cold War insurrections in the 1990s rekindled interests in demographic factors among defense and intelligence analysts, and stimulated the publication of an extensive range of analyses, including technical reports published by RAND, the American Association for the Advancement of Science, the International Crisis Group, and the Environmental Change and Security Project of the Woodrow Wilson Center for International Scholars.[3] Regarded as non-traditional security issues just a decade ago, the implications of population trends today figure prominently in global analyses published by Britain's Ministry of Defence, in landmark security assessments published in the United States by the Central Intelligence Agency's Strategic Assessment Group, and by the National Intelligence Council.[4]

Content

The report's first chapter briefly reviews the recent history of civil conflict and the puzzling early finding that high levels of infant mortality were associated with outbreaks of civil conflict and other serious forms of political instability. The second chapter reviews the demographic transition and presents evidence of a correspondence between a country's progress through this transition and a subsequent decline in its risk of civil conflict. Succeeding chapters review possible mechanisms for that change, focusing on four *demographic stress factors* currently observed to varying degrees in countries now in the early and middle stages of their demographic transition: a large proportion of young adults, rapid growth of urban population, exceptionally low per capita availability of cropland and renewable fresh water, and a high rate of death among working-age adults—a major consequence of the HIV/AIDS pandemic. In each of these chapters, recent research on a demographic stress factor is reviewed, and its numerical correspondence to civil conflict in the 1990s is tested. Each chapter utilizes world maps to portray the geographical distribution of the stress factor in 2005. The final chapter of the report discusses interactions among these demographic stress factors, and presents an analysis of the demographic risks of civil conflict over the current decade. Each chapter closes with a set of briefing points designed to review and summarize the preceding material.

Our research builds on data collected by specialists in the fields of both armed conflict and population. The Conflict Data Project, based at Uppsala University in Sweden, provided data on the location, timing and intensity of recent armed conflicts.[5] Population data are from the most recent estimates and projections of the United Nations Population Division.[6] Appendices elaborate further on data and methodologies. They include bibliographic endnotes; a glossary of key terms [Appendix 1]; data sources and methodologies [A.2]; a list of figures, their data sources, and methodological and statistical notes [A.3]; and a country-by-country listing of data used in the analysis of the risk of civil conflict in the current decade (2000 to 2010) [A.4].

Both its brevity and its focus require that this report omit a review of theories explaining the process by which civil conflicts emerge, and that it skip lightly over the non-demographic factors that arguably influence the stability of nation-states. Among these are democratization,[7] economic development and the alleviation of poverty,[8] openness to trade and other facets of globalization,[9] and the national and international conditions facilitating conflict mediation.[10] To minimize the occurrence and deadly costs of armed conflict, governments need to address as many of the acknowledged risk factors as possible. And while this report focuses squarely on demographic risks of civil conflict, it is clear that governance, economics and the international political environment also can impart substantial risks as well as interact with demographic processes.

What is the Security Demographic?

The term employed as the title of this report—the *security demographic*—embodies a set of stability-promoting demographic characteristics that typify populations near the end of their demographic transition. Over the past two decades, some 20 developing countries have taken on these features by attaining low birth and death rates. Most have done so by pursuing policies and supporting programs that increased their citizens' access to primary—and specifically to reproductive—health care, and to education.

Why should analysts and security policymakers interest themselves in policies and programs that alter demographic outcomes? The evidence presented in this report suggests strongly that helping countries approach the final phase of demographic transition—a phase in which people live long lives and families are typically small, healthy and educated, where population age structure is mature and population growth is nearly at its end—promises ultimately to reduce the frequency of civil conflicts and to help bring about a more peaceful world.

CHAPTER ONE

Conflicts and Conundrums

The fall of the Berlin Wall in 1989 and the dissolution of the Soviet Union two years later brought hopes for a *peace dividend*—a benefit from the drop in defense spending anticipated in countries once locked into what seemed an unending face-off between the Warsaw Pact states and their NATO opponents. Some experts fully expected the release of tensions in Europe to favor political stability in Asia, Africa and Latin America. The industrialized powers would spend more on foreign aid and cease sponsoring military regimes or their insurgent rivals. Funds once spent on the maintenance of oversized security forces in developing countries would shift to social and economic programs. Or so the hope was.

The dividend, however, never materialized. The fear of nuclear war faded, only to be replaced almost immediately by a new concern: rising numbers of *civil conflicts*—revolutions, ethnic wars, terrorist attacks and state-sponsored violence occurring within states. [See endnote on the term *state*.][11] To finance their insurgencies, militant organizations drew from a mix of illicit sources, including kidnapping and extortion, illegal trade in gems and narcotics, assistance from rogue states and so-called religious charities, and from sympathetic emigrants living in industrial countries.[12] Internal conflicts are the principal means by which military and political strongmen have seized power and achieved the authority to roll back democratization and seize capital. As such, they arguably pose the most formidable obstruction to economic development in sub-Saharan Africa and in parts of Asia and Latin America.[13]

The frequency of civil war, which had climbed steadily throughout the Cold War era, surged upward again in the early 1990s [Figure 1.1]. In 1992 the world reached a post-World War II peak of

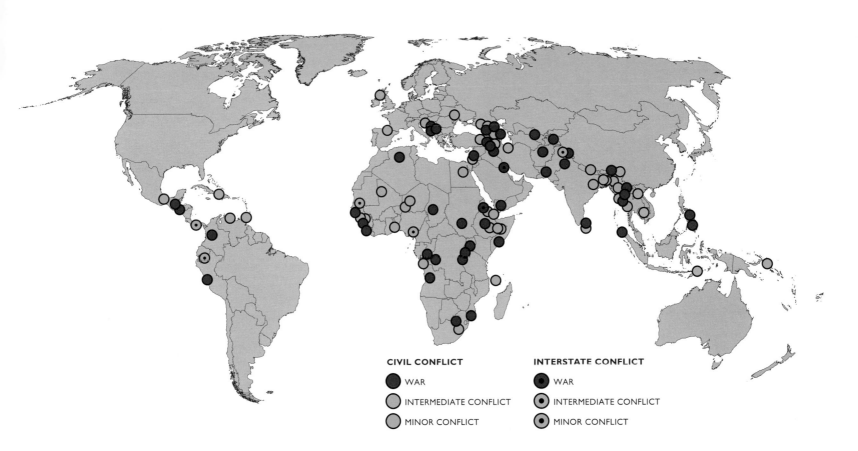

CIVIL CONFLICT
- ● WAR
- ◐ INTERMEDIATE CONFLICT
- ○ MINOR CONFLICT

INTERSTATE CONFLICT
- ● WAR
- ◉ INTERMEDIATE CONFLICT
- ◉ MINOR CONFLICT

55 active armed conflicts. All but one were civil conflicts. And while the 1990s ended with a declining trend in the annual frequency of active armed conflicts—probably the outcome both of successful mediation and the suppression of small-scale and incipient conflicts—it was a record decade for bloodshed: 107 armed conflicts [Map 1] were active in 63 states, more conflicts and more states than in any of the previous four decades [conflict data discussed in Appendix 2A], leaving behind more than 2.5 million dead.[14]

Alarmed at conflict trends in the early 1990s, intelligence analysts and academics initiated a series of studies designed to identify and explore the underlying conditions putting states at risk of civil violence and insurrection. Researchers identified several non-demographic risks: States only midway on the journey to full democracy were often unstable. Governments that restricted trade and the flow of capital tended to face political upheaval. And low- and middle-income states with economies excessively dependent on the harvest of raw natural resources such as petroleum, precious minerals, or high-priced timber were often especially fragile—vulnerable to the rise of insurgents financed by extortion and illegal trade.[15]

However, the number and prominence of demographic risk factors suggested by this research drew considerable attention. The findings rekindled analysts' interest in conflict-related population studies of previous decades and stimulated further research. The chapters that follow draw upon this foundation. But some of the demographic risk factors that emerged from conflict research during the 1990s were unexpected. One in particular was gnawingly puzzling.

MAP 1

ARMED CONFLICTS, 1990–2000

The map shows the general location of the civil and interstate conflicts that occurred from 1990 to 2000, and the maximum intensity that each achieved in that period. A minor conflict claimed at least 25 battle-related deaths per year, but fewer than 1,000 deaths during its entire course. An intermediate conflict accumulated at least 1,000 deaths, with fewer than 1,000 dying each year. War resulted in at least 1,000 deaths during a single year.

DATA SOURCE: WALLENSTEEN AND SOLLENBERG, 2001

FIGURE 1.1

THE ANNUAL NUMBER OF CIVIL AND INTER-STATE CONFLICTS, 1946–2001

Civil conflicts greatly outnumber interstate conflicts. Since the 1950s, the number of interstate conflicts (warfare between the governments of two or more countries) has shown no upward or downward trend, while civil conflicts more than doubled, peaking in the early 1990s.

DATA SOURCES: GLEDITSCH ET AL., 2002; WALLENSTEEN AND SOLLENBERG, 2001

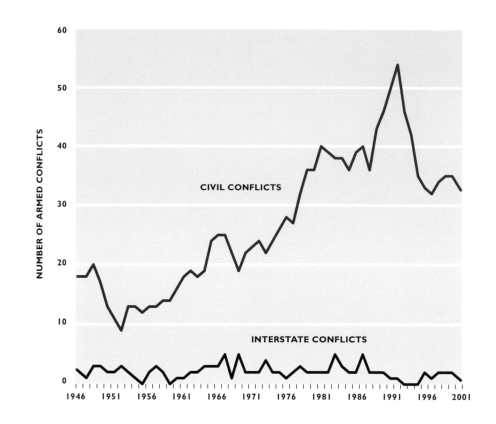

The Infant Mortality Conundrum

For nearly a decade, intelligence analysts and political scientists have squabbled over the significance of a seemingly straightforward demographic and health indicator: the *infant mortality rate* (the proportion of newborns dying before they reach their first birthday, expressed as a number of deaths per thousand live births). At the core of this contention is a set of research results published during the 1990s by a group of consultants to the U.S. Central Intelligence Agency known as the State Failure Task Force. This team of U.S. political scientists and statisticians employed computer-aided statistical methods to sift through hundreds of social, political, economic, and environmental variables, from the mid-1950s to the mid-1990s, looking for factors that could predict a phenomenon they labeled *state failure*—a collapse of national order caused by mass political or ethnic killings, coups d'état, and civil wars.[16] The group found high rates of infant mortality to be the best single predictor of these events worldwide, and an even better predictor in a model that also included a lack of openness to trade and low levels of democracy.

The infant mortality rate, however, is not the only demographic factor with strong statistical links to conflict. In the late 1960s, historian Herbert Moller noted that the most conflict-prone European states of the 19th and early 20th centuries tended to have unusually large proportions of people in their late teens and twenties.[17] Since then, a series of historical and contemporary studies has linked the predominance of young adults to unusually high incidence and severity of warfare in strife-ridden regions of the world (discussed in Chapter 3).[18]

This report shows these two parallel paths of research to be sides of the same coin. Taken together, a high rate of infant mortality and a large proportion of youth are indicative of populations in the early and middle stages of *demographic transition*. This transformation—the pace of which has been accelerated in many developing countries by international funding, particularly maternal and child health services and family planning programs—is the change in populations from low to high chances of child survival and from large to small families, and thus from high to low rates of both birth and death. A comparison of demographic and civil conflict data in the 1990–2000 period, explored in the pages that follow, demonstrates that certain characteristics of these early and middle stages of the demographic transition, such as especially youthful populations and rapid urban population growth, can add to the political instability of states and ultimately to their vulnerability to violent civil unrest. Moving to the late stages of the transition, the data indicate, tends to reduce the risk that new civil conflicts will emerge.

As a stabilizing process in nation-states, progress along the demographic transition receives much less recognition and research focus from most quarters of the security community than promotion of democracy and market reforms. This may be an error. In recent years some analysts (discussed in the following chapter) have argued that, in the absence of major social changes, pushing democratization and economic liberalization can inspire civil unrest. As the next chapter explains, the suite of policies and programs that help countries pass through the demographic transition may facilitate the type of social changes that are necessary to achieve peaceful democratic and economic transitions.

■ **KEY POINT** Analysts recently have determined that, throughout the latter half of the 20th century, high rates of infant mortality consistently were associated with the emergence of civil conflicts. Others have pointed to the importance of large proportions in populations of young adults in the emergence and intensity of armed conflict and insurrection, particularly where opportunities for individual economic and social advancement have been constrained.

■ **KEY POINT** The focal points of these theses—high rates of infant mortality and large proportions of youth—are, placed together, signature characteristics of populations in the early stages of their demographic transition. The analyses in this report set out to determine the degree to which progress through this transition influences the vulnerability of countries to civil conflict, and to examine the most plausible explanations for those influences.

■ **POLICY PRESCRIPTION** Greater recognition of the demographic transition as a security-relevant process could inspire researchers to delve deeper into relationships between demographic factors and armed conflict and encourage policymakers to become familiar with the foreign policies and international programs that have influenced the speed of demographic transition.

BRIEFING POINTS Demographic Change and Armed Conflict

CHAPTER TWO

Transition from Turmoil

MAPS 2.1 AND 2.2

Opposite: In the early 1970s, women in almost every developing country were estimated to have, on average, more than four children during their lives. In the three decades that followed, a revolution in childbearing spread across the world. Yet progress along the demographic transition has been uneven and lags in several regions.

DATA SOURCE: UNITED NATIONS POPULATION DIVISION, 2003

About one-third of all countries are in the latter stage of what demographers call the *demographic transition*—the transformation of a population characterized by short lives and large families to one with long lives and small families. These 65 or so countries, all with low rates of birth and death, contain half the world's population and much more than half of its wealth.[19] The first signs of this historic transition arose in northern Europe in the mid-18th century, with a slow but steady reduction in the risk that the average person would die in early childhood and/or as the casualty of an epidemic infectious disease.[20] Why did the risk of early death decline? The reasons vary, from simple improvements in personal hygiene that came with the wider availability of soap to discoveries in medical science and agricultural technologies. These advances were, in part, facilitated by the growing financial power of European states and the expanding organizational capacity of their bureaucracies. Slow but steady declines in European birth rates followed about a century later, for reasons and through means that demographers still debate. Birth rates continue to drift downward in Europe today to levels that worry some analysts. Such trends are leading many countries to current or future population decrease that only high levels of immigration might offset.[21]

In most Asian, Caribbean and Latin American countries, comparable declines in childhood mortality began only in the early to mid-20th century, and declines in birth rates began only in the mid-1960s and 1970s. For both rates, however, the pace of decline has been unprecedentedly swift: the transitions that most European countries took about 150 years to complete occurred in parts of East Asia and the Caribbean in less than 50 years. Recent research provides substantial evidence that girls' education [Figure 2.1], later marriage, and women's employment outside the home have played

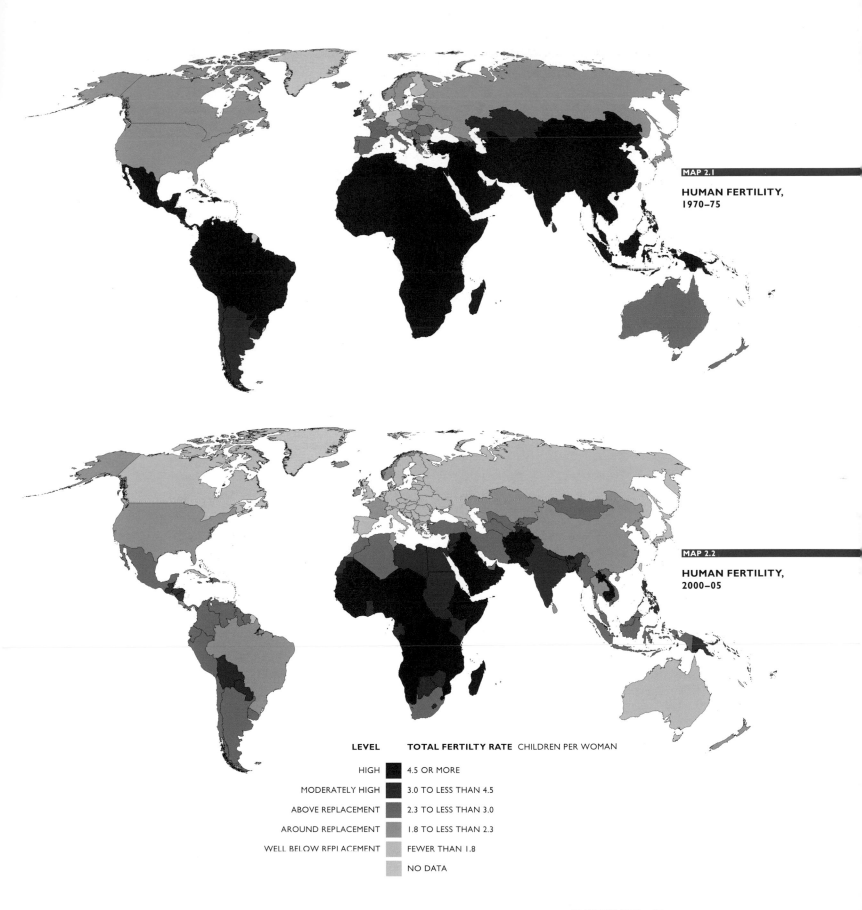

MAP 2.1

HUMAN FERTILITY,
1970–75

MAP 2.2

HUMAN FERTILITY,
2000–05

LEVEL	TOTAL FERTILTY RATE CHILDREN PER WOMAN
HIGH	4.5 OR MORE
MODERATELY HIGH	3.0 TO LESS THAN 4.5
ABOVE REPLACEMENT	2.3 TO LESS THAN 3.0
AROUND REPLACEMENT	1.8 TO LESS THAN 2.3
WELL BELOW REPLACEMENT	FEWER THAN 1.8
	NO DATA

FIGURE 2.1

THE RELATIONSHIP BETWEEN WOMEN'S EDUCATION AND FERTILITY, 1995–2000

In general, the longer a girl remains in school, the fewer births she is likely to have. Some of the regional variation in this relationship is probably due to the differences in women's economic opportunities provided by attaining higher levels of education, and differences in the trade-offs (what economists call opportunity costs) in terms of childbearing that are needed to realize those opportunities. Some variation may be produced by regional differences in the amount of control women have over decisions related to childbearing, and regional differences in their access to affordable contraception.

DATA SOURCES: LUTZ AND GOUJON, 2001; FROM VARIOUS DEMOGRAPHIC AND HEALTH SURVEYS

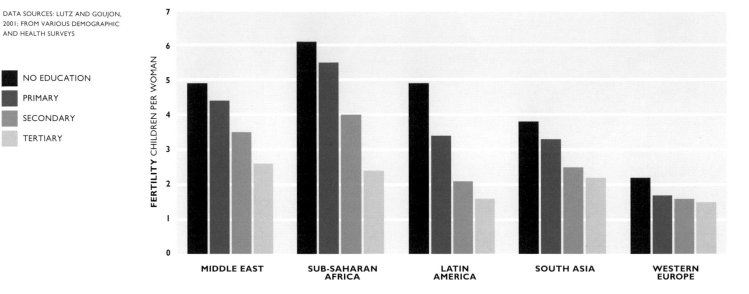

■ NO EDUCATION
■ PRIMARY
■ SECONDARY
■ TERTIARY

important roles in improving childhood nutrition, deterring childhood mortality, and increasing the demand for contraception.[22] Patterns of modern decline in fertility correspond closely to increased use of modern contraception [Figure 2.2]. And the results of national and local studies suggest that declines in both fertility and childhood mortality have reinforced each other.[23]

In certain regions of the world, however, most countries have made far less progress along the demographic transition. More than one-third of all countries (about 1.5 billion people) remain in the transition's early and middle phases.[24] That is, rates of birth and death—particularly the deaths of infants, children and women in pregnancy and childbirth—remain high in most of sub-Saharan Africa and in parts of South and Central Asia. And birth rates remain high despite relatively low death rates in much of the Middle East and in several Latin American countries and Pacific Islands.

Moreover, a new, demographically significant force has emerged in the last 25 years, unforeseen by those who first developed the model of the demographic transition. Death rates have actually reversed their decline in more than 30 countries, most in sub-Saharan Africa, due largely to the HIV/AIDS pandemic. In some formerly communist Eastern European countries, rising death rates involve other aspects of declining public health, such as increasing alcoholism and tobacco use, a tuberculosis epidemic, environmental health problems, and a roll-back in the quality of affordable health services.[25] In a few countries—notably Rwanda and East Timor—recent civil conflicts themselves boosted death rates significantly.

By themselves, annual rates of birth and death seem like the driest and most basic of all national statistics. Working together over time, however, birth and death rates—along with migration rates where they are substantial—set powerful demographic forces into play. Population growth or decline, domestic demand for food, fresh water and energy, *urbanization* (increasing proportions of a population in and around cities), and international migration all fall under the sway of birth and death rates. Trends in birth, death and migration determine a population's *age structure* (the proportions of people in each age group relative to the population as a whole), which in turn determines the ratio of dependents to economically active people, the relative size of the school-age population, and the numbers of those entering and leaving the workforce. Clearly, any one of these forces can exert a vast array of political, social, economic, and environmental influences upon society.

Demographic Transition and Civil Conflict

But are forces coupled to the demographic transition powerful enough to influence a nation-state's vulnerability to civil conflict? The results of the following analysis suggests that they are—that countries in the earlier stages of the transition are at greater risk than those near its end, and most importantly, that moving through the transition gradually reduces that risk. The claim made here is not that demographic processes act alone in raising or reducing the chances of political instabilities. Nor does population change lead directly or inevitably to conflict. Researchers who have studied the evolution of civil conflict almost universally describe it as a complex, multi-stage process.[26] This process builds upon a state's historic and current vulnerabilities, and is driven over time by largely country-specific and unpredictable events. Yet a significant and much underrated proportion of these vulnerabilities, the data presented here strongly suggest, result from a population's position and pace through the demographic transition.

Our conclusions are based on analyses of civil conflict in the 1970s, '80s and '90s. Our primary focus is on the 1990s—a time period, devoid of superpower tensions, comprising security challenges that are likely to resemble those that could arise in the early decades of the 21st century—using data assembled by the Conflict Data Project at the University of Uppsala.[27] For each of the three decades of analysis, the demographic status of countries, in terms of birth and death rates (expressing the number of these events per thousand people in the population), is characterized using United Nations population data from the period directly preceding the decade to best characterize the demographic background for the decade's events. For example, in the analysis of the 1990s, birth and death rates from the second half of the '80s are used to characterize the demographic status of countries [Appendix 3B-C]. Our analyses each begin by considering all countries with populations greater than 150,000 (about 180 countries). But because of the need to filter out persistent and recurring conflicts (discussed below), and changes in the status of states, the actual count of countries used in calculations in these analyses varies (118–145 countries) [see Appendix 2D].

The relation between the demographic transition and conflict is tested for newly initiated conflicts, which we label *outbreaks of civil conflict*; not insurrections that were carried over from the final five years of the previous decade. Why this restriction? Because, as peacekeepers can report, where there has been recent conflict—where blood has been spilled, where weapons are accessible, and where leaders still live off the spoils of war—countries remain highly vulnerable to recurrent warfare.[28] And when civil war persists, as it has for decades in Afghanistan, India's state of Kashmir and Colombia, the relationships between social conditions, economic trends and conflict can be

FIGURE 2.2

THE RELATIONSHIP BETWEEN CONTRACEPTIVE USE AND FERTILITY DECLINE, 1995–2000

As the percentage of married women of reproductive age using contraceptives has increased, the total fertility rate (children per woman) has declined. Each data point marks the position of a country's population in terms of contraceptive use and fertility, from 1995–2000. According to this relationship, an increase of 15 percent in the proportion of married women using modern methods of contraception leads to a 1-child decline in fertility. Several Eastern European and former-Soviet states that deviate significantly from this relationship, exhibiting low fertility and low contraceptive use (lower left corner of the graph). In these countries, women have used abortion to manage fertility in the absence of adequate and affordable family planning services.

APPENDIX 3 FOR STATISTICAL RELATIONSHIP; DATA SOURCES: POPULATION ACTION INTERNATIONAL, 1998, FROM VARIOUS SOURCES, UN POPULATION DIVISION, 2003

- EASTERN EUROPE AND FORMER SOVIET UNION
- WESTERN EUROPE AND OTHER INDUSTRIALIZED COUNTRIES
- MIDDLE EAST AND NORTH AFRICA
- SUB-SAHARAN AFRICA
- LATIN AMERICA AND THE CARIBBEAN
- SOUTH AND EAST ASIA
- ALL COUNTRIES (ON AVERAGE)

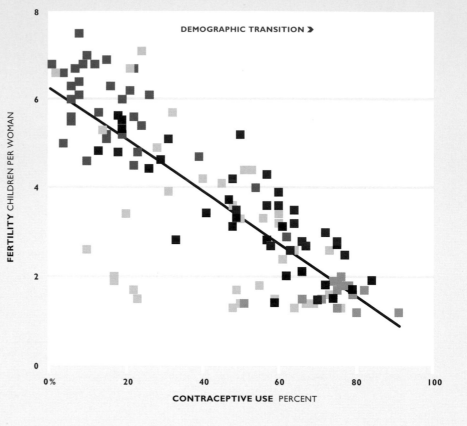

FIGURE 2.3

COUNTRIES WITH OUTBREAKS OF CIVIL CONFLICT, 1990–2000: THEIR POSITIONS ALONG THE PATH OF DEMOGRAPHIC TRANSITION

The likelihood of experiencing an outbreak of civil conflict in the 1990s was highest for countries in the early and middle phases of demographic transition. Each point represents a country, in terms of its birth and death rate (measured as the number of events per 1,000 people), 1985–1990. The curved line traces the general path of countries as they proceeded along the demographic transition during the late 1980s, at the close of the Cold War. During the next decade, most countries in civil conflict were situated left of the curve's trough. Few countries to the right, in the vicinity of population equilibrium (diagonal dotted line), experienced an outbreak of civil conflict.

APPENDIX 3 FOR STATISTICAL RELATIONSHIP; DATA SOURCE: UN POPULATION DIVISION, 2003; GLEDITSCH ET AL. 2002; WALLENSTEEN AND SOLLENBERG, 2001

- COUNTRY WITH AN OUTBREAK OF CIVIL CONFLICT
- COUNTRY WITHOUT AN OUTBREAK OF CIVIL CONFLICT
- ALL COUNTRIES (ON AVERAGE)
- --- WHERE BIRTHS EQUAL DEATHS

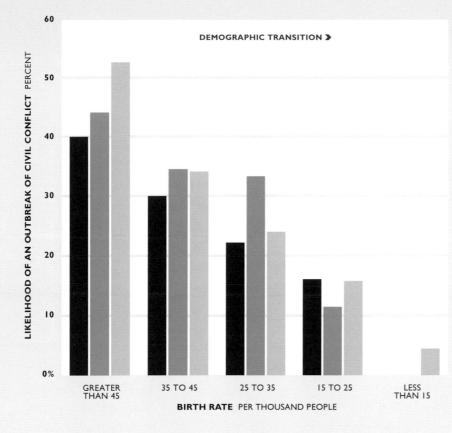

DEMOGRAPHIC TRANSITION ➤

LIKELIHOOD OF AN OUTBREAK OF CIVIL CONFLICT PERCENT

BIRTH RATE PER THOUSAND PEOPLE

GREATER THAN 45 · 35 TO 45 · 25 TO 35 · 15 TO 25 · LESS THAN 15

FIGURE 2.4

RELATIONSHIP BETWEEN DEMOGRAPHIC TRANSITION AND THE LIKELIHOOD OF CIVIL CONFLICT, 1970S, '80S AND '90S

Decline in the likelihood of civil conflict mirrored progress along the demographic transition, from the 1970s through the 1990s. During the 1970s and '80s, however, only a handful of developing countries had made substantial progress through the demographic transition, and Eastern and Southern European countries had not yet reached the low rates of birth (annual births per 1,000 people) currently experienced.

DATA SOURCES: GLEDITSCH ET AL. 2002; UNITED NATIONS POPULATION DIVISION, 2003

■ 1970 TO 1980

■ 1980 TO 1990

■ 1990 TO 2000

PRE-TRANSITION · EARLY TRANSITION · MIDDLE TRANSITION · LATE TRANSITION · POST-TRANSITION

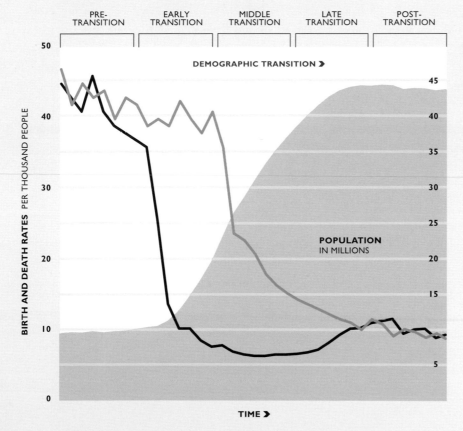

DEMOGRAPHIC TRANSITION ➤

BIRTH AND DEATH RATES PER THOUSAND PEOPLE

POPULATION IN MILLIONS

TIME ➤

FIGURE 2.5

THE PROCESS OF DEMOGRAPHIC TRANSITION: AN IDEALIZED MODEL

The graph portrays idealized paths of the demographic transition's two component transitions—birth-rate and death-rate transitions—and shows resulting population growth. All countries are going through this process or have passed through it. Individually, birth-rate and death-rate transitions have taken from 50 to 150 years to complete. Some developing countries are passing through these transitions very rapidly, much faster than European or North American countries did. Population growth and decline are results of gaps between birth rates and death rates (measured per thousand people). Because death rates typically decrease before birth rates begin to decline, population tends to grow rapidly during the transition.

▬ BIRTH RATE

▬ DEATH RATE

▬ POPULATION

virtually impossible to untangle. In this analysis, the likelihood of civil conflict was calculated as the proportion of countries in a category (delineated by a range of birth rates) that experienced a new outbreak of civil conflict, at any level of intensity, during the decade. This calculation disregarded countries engaged in a persistent or recurring civil conflict that was active in the five years directly preceding the decade [for methods, see Appendix 2D].

After persistent and recurrent conflicts were filtered out, our analysis of the 1990s found that progress through the demographic transition was associated with a consistent and steady decline in the risk of civil conflict [Figure 2.3 and Table 2.1]. By the '90s, more than two dozen developing countries had progressed to medium-to-low rates of birth and death. Most of these countries were in the Caribbean, East Asian and Southeast Asian regions. Several late-transition countries that experienced episodes of sporadic student-led violence or armed insurrections as early-transition countries in the decades following World War II—such as Thailand, South Korea, Tunisia and Malaysia— remained stable during the 1990s despite outbreaks of conflict around them.

While this trend toward decreasing vulnerability among states passing through the demographic transition is active regionally and globally, there are individual examples of countries that demonstrate that demographic risk does not inevitably lead to civil conflict. Governance, economic policies, and conflict resolution mediate those risks. For example, Cape Verde (in West Africa), a demographically high-risk state in the 1980s and 1990s, may have offset its vulnerability by facilitating labor migration to Europe and encouraging remittances. Others, like Tanzania and Brazil, distributed farmland. Oil-rich states created urban employment, large armies and bloated bureaucracies, and ruthlessly repressed dissent when even these measures failed. And it is not clear that the demographic transition can do much, by itself, to stop persistent and recurring warfare. In a few countries where progress along the demographic transition should have helped alleviate risk—such as Colombia, Northern Ireland (United Kingdom) and Sri Lanka—costly civil conflicts that first

---

TABLE 2.1

THE RELATIONSHIP BETWEEN BIRTHS, INFANT DEATHS AND THE LIKELIHOOD OF CIVIL CONFLICT, 1990–2000

High birth and infant mortality rates in countries were associated with a high likelihood of an outbreak of civil conflict during the 1990s. And, as birth rates (annual births per 1,000 people in a population) and infant mortality rates (annual infant deaths per 1,000 live births) became progressively lower, so did the likelihood of civil conflict. The infant mortality rates in the table are the average of this measure in the countries falling in the birth rate categories listed to their left.

DATA SOURCES: WALLENSTEEN AND SOLLENBERG, 2001; UNITED NATIONS POPULATION DIVISION, 2003

Birth Rate 1985-90 Annual Births Per Thousand People	Average Infant Mortality Rate 1985-90 Annual Infant Deaths Per Thousand Live Births	Likelihood of an Outbreak of Civil Conflict 1990-2000
45.0 or more	125	53%
35.0 to 44.9	78	34%
25.0 to 34.9	42	24%
15.0 to 24.9	20	16%
Less than 15.0	10	5%

emerged decades before, at earlier stages of transition, were still active through parts of the 1990s. There is speculation, however, that the demographic transition's effects on age structure and work-force growth (discussed below) are improving the chances of success for peace negotiations occurring in Northern Ireland and Sri Lanka.

The demographic transition's influence on the world's states, as a group, has been both impressive and sustained. Risk was highest among countries that entered the 1990s with very high birth rates (greater than or equal to 45 births per thousand people) and relatively high infant mortality rates.[29] Nearly half of the countries in this category experienced a new conflict. And declines in birth rates and infant mortality rates corresponded closely to declines in the risk of armed conflict. A decline in the birth rate of five births per thousand people corresponded to a decline of just over 5 percent in the risk of civil conflict. A further analysis of the 1970s and 1980s shows that there were similar transition-related effects during those Cold War decades [Figure 2.4].

This evidence suggests that a country's level of progress along the demographic transition can influence the global security environment. The findings themselves however, shed little light on what the mechanisms of influence might be; rather, they beg important questions for national security policymakers and analysts. For example, what early- and middle-transition forces might make states more vulnerable to civil unrest? Are those processes truly demographic, or are demographic changes a simple reflection of changes that are occurring in economics and governance? Much of what follows attempts to answer these critical questions.

The Demographic Transition in Brief

A better understanding of the demographic transition suggests what the answer might be. Although the transition is a continuous process, it may be best understood as a succession of five phases. All of today's countries have already emerged from the first of these—the *pre-transition phase*, which dominated most of human history. In this phase women fortunate enough to survive their reproductive years typically experienced many live births, but half or more of these children died before age five. Because global human population grew very slowly until a few centuries ago, demographers assume that few populations living before the modern era ever moved beyond the pre-transition phase. This assumption is supported by historical, archeological and anthropological research indicating that infant and maternal mortality tended to be much higher, and average adult lifespan much shorter than today.[30]

Today, all countries belong in one of the next four phases: the *early-transition*, *middle-transition*, *late-transition*, and *post-transition phases* [Figure 2.5]. A population's progress through these phases is most easily understood in terms of two components: birth rates and death rates. The adjoining maps [Map 2.1, 2.2], however, are color-coded using a single, more straightforward measure: a country's *total fertility rate*, which is an estimate of the average number of live births per woman during her lifetime, and a reasonable gauge of the average family size. Of particular interest to analysts who track recent population dynamics are the countries near *replacement fertility*—the level of slightly more than two children per woman at which populations would ultimately level off and stop growing in the absence of migration, assuming low mortality rates throughout the childhood and the reproductive years.

Progress in nutrition, sanitation, and prevention and treatment of infectious disease have historically brought populations into a second stage of the demographic transition—the *early-transition phase*, during which childhood death rates decline while birth rates remain high. Birth rates have tended to decrease less readily than death rates not only because of cultural preferences for many children and long lives, but also because techniques for preventing unwanted pregnancy have tended to be more complicated, less diverse and much more controversial than those available for extending life. The gap that develops between birth and death rates in this early stage of transition produces several important demographic features. Perhaps the most notable is rapid population growth, but other outcomes are unusually large proportions of children and adolescent dependents and a relative dearth of working age adults per dependent. (At this stage of the transition, elderly dependents typically comprise a very small proportion of the population, usually less than 3 percent.)

The *middle phase* of the demographic transition is typified by decreasing family size and a shift to a more mature age structure [Figures 2.6A, B and C]. In recent decades, this phase has coincided with an upsurge in the use of modern contraception, and often has been characterized by elongated delays before marriage and before girls end schooling, and falling rates of pregnancy-related deaths. Declines in fertility begin to advance the population's *median age* (the age at which the number of those older is exactly equal to those younger). Unless substantial migration intervenes, the population growth rate slows. However, birth rates typically remain far above death rates and population continues to climb.

Further population growth and maturation of the age structure continue in the *late-transition phase*. As fertility approaches the two-child-per-woman level, youth become a smaller proportion of the population than in earlier phases, and the elderly begin to comprise a larger proportion. Death rates rise, reflecting a slow increase in the diseases of old age, away from the high incidence of childhood illnesses common in earlier phases. Until late-transition populations acquire a more mature age structure, death rates tend to remain lower than birth rates. This phenomenon, which demographers call *population momentum*, can extend population growth for four to six decades after replacement fertility is reached. And this momentum is currently the major source of population growth in numerous countries that, within the last several decades, attained fertility levels near-replacement or below—including China (total fertility rate of 1.8 children per woman, in 2000–05), Iran (2.3 children per woman), Tunisia (2.0), Indonesia (2.3), Vietnam (2.3), Thailand (1.9), and Brazil (2.2).[31]

The demographic future is unclear for countries in the *post-transition phase*, where the momentum of population growth has run its course. One post-transitional characteristic is a near certainty: that the population's elderly proportion will grow larger than ever before—commonly to around one-fifth of the whole, according to UN projections. In some cases this proportion could become higher than one-third, at least temporarily. Population decline is a possibility throughout the industrial world, and a current reality in more than a dozen countries, including Russia, Italy and much of Eastern Europe. Due to decades of below-replacement-level fertility, the age structures of some European countries are likely to lead (in the absence of major increases in migration) to population decline over the next several decades—a phenomenon demographers call *negative population momentum*.[32]

Population decline can also be the outgrowth of rising death rates. The still-growing HIV/AIDS pandemic is the major cause of reversals in mortality trends today. According to the UN Population Division, three of the countries most severely affected by AIDS—Botswana, South Africa and Lesotho—all with birth rates typical of middle-transition countries, could experience population decline before 2010.

Isn't It Just Economic Progress and Good Governance?

The society-changing, state-building influences of the demographic transition are notoriously difficult to unravel from other aspects of national progress. To the casual observer, development seems to occur on many fronts at roughly the same time—and for a reason: demographic transition, sound economic fundamentals and responsible governance promote each other, generating a "virtuous cycle" of development (detailed in the following section of this chapter on the "demographic bonus"). Yet, according to a number of recent analyses, rapid economic liberalization and democratization can destabilize countries, particularly if they occur without basic societal changes, which we contend are made easier by a society-wide shift to small, well-educated, healthy families and longer lives, or evolve hand-in-hand with this transition.

Perhaps the most coherent critique of "free-market democracy in a vacuum," is rendered by Yale Law School professor Amy Chua, who argues that in many low and middle-income countries business wealth has become heavily concentrated in the hands of a proportionally small group of families of ethnic minorities who, through cultural channels of reciprocity, help each other divide up markets and accumulate capital.[33] While fast-paced democratic and free-market reforms are viewed hopefully from the West, in these countries they can be destabilizing—allowing well-financed minorities to control larger shares of the business and finance political campaigns, or paving the way for populist demagogues to ride a wave of ethnic animosity to power.

Statistical studies support this thesis, concluding that partially democratized states—now totaling about one-third of all states worldwide[34]—have been inordinately susceptible to the cycle of state failure and civil conflict, particularly those that have abruptly changed to a more democratic regime during the past 10 years.[35] These findings lend credence to the hypothesis that the *Asian Tiger model of development* [Figure 2.7A and B], whereby substantial progress along the demographic transition precedes or occurs simultaneously with incremental free-market reforms and democratization[36]—discussed below—represents a more secure development model than the rapid imposition of free-market democracy.

Transition's Opportunities: The Demographic Bonus

Where the demographic transition is in its latter phases, societies face opportunities and challenges attributable to the transition's effects on age structure. As fertility nears the replacement level, small families become common and working-age adults assume a large proportion of the population. These trends encourage household savings, lessen the burdens on public schools and other government services, increase the number of taxable adults per dependent, and help families invest more in each child. Some economists refer to this one-time bulge in the workforce and simultaneous rise in the support ratio—the number of working-age adults per child—as a *demographic bonus*.[37]

EXAMPLES OF POPULATION AGE STRUCTURES AT PROGRESSIVE STAGES OF DEMOGRAPHIC TRANSITION

The populations of countries, such as Afghanistan, that are in the early phase of the demographic transition typically have age structures that exhibit a predominance of young adults (commonly called a youth bulge) and children. As countries advance into the late phase of transition—shown by the population age structure of South Korea—the proportion of children begins to drop off, but a youth bulge persists for a decade or two, moving "upward" into the older age classes. France's population has a more mature age structure, typical of populations that have passed through the demographic transition into the post-transition phase.

DATA SOURCE: UNITED NATIONS POPULATION DIVISION, 2003

FIGURE 2.6 A

AFGHANISTAN IN 2000

An Early-transition
Population

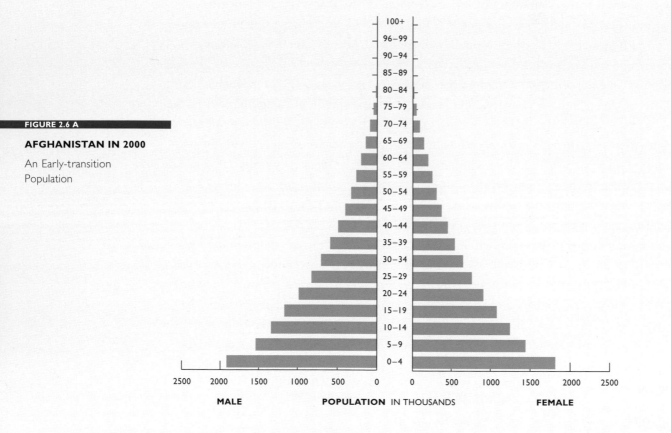

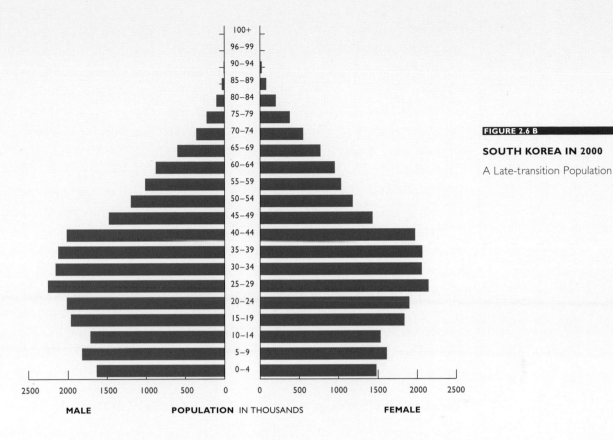

FIGURE 2.6 B

SOUTH KOREA IN 2000

A Late-transition Population

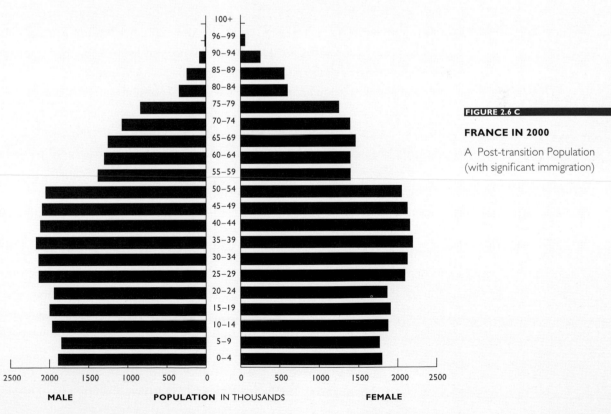

FIGURE 2.6 C

FRANCE IN 2000

A Post-transition Population
(with significant immigration)

In the 1960s and early 1970s, states in East and Southeast Asia (including South Korea, Thailand, Taiwan, Malaysia and Indonesia) expanded access to public education and primary health and family planning services. Fertility declined rapidly over the ensuing decades. People lived longer, married later in life and, with smaller families, saved a relatively large portion of their wages and spent more on educating each child. When labor force growth began to slow in the late 1980s, wages rose. Attracted by the pay, women entered the manufacturing workforce in large numbers.[38] Then fertility declined again.

As their labor forces grew increasingly educated and urbanized, these states—which economists dubbed the Asian Tigers—adjusted their business and trade policies to encourage investments from technologically advanced manufacturing industries in North America and Japan. Authors of a recent economic review of this phenomenon attribute about one-third of the Tigers' 6 percent annual average economic growth per capita, over a period stretching from the mid-1960s through the early 1990s, to the effects of advantageous age structures.[39] Endowed with unusually high savings rates, the Asian Tigers actually exported financial capital to the West until they were hit by a regional economic downdraft in the late 1990s. Today other developing countries that have recently attained late-transition status — including Sri Lanka, Mexico, China, Iran, Tunisia and Vietnam — have evolved age structures that are favorable to economic growth. And this development could help ease civil tensions where they exist.[40]

Transition's Challenges: Aging and the Possibility of Decline

Some economists and demographers are alarmed by the prospect of deleterious effects on social cohesion and economic prosperity from a post-transitional aging population and decline in the size of the workforce. This is uncertain terrain. Industrial countries are just beginning to grapple with the challenges of a shrinking workforce and a large and growing proportion of the elderly. So far, none have shown overt signs of unusual economic or political instability because of it—including Russia, where the median age has risen to 38 years and population is declining by around 1 million people (0.7 percent) annually. Inevitably, all states must face some degree of demographic challenge as they approach population stability or experience population decline. And, in contrast to the minimal capacity of many developing countries to adjust to continuing rapid population growth, industrial countries have considerable capacity to adjust to aging and decline in population.

Some adjustment is already occurring. Confronted with a growing proportion of elderly, some European states have worked to maintain lower ratios of workers to retirees by accepting more immigrants, extending the retirement age, and attracting more women into the workforce while making it easier for them to raise children while working. Japan, while reluctant to accept a large number of immigrants, is experimenting with several of these options, as well as returning some of the responsibility for elder care to families.[41] To deal with a shrinking workforce, Japan is continuing to replace low-skill jobs with technology and to move its less innovative, labor-intense industries overseas. The Japanese government has committed to worker re-training programs and stepped up investments in research and development.[42]

Despite these policy responses, it would be unwise to dismiss future population aging or decline as inconsequential. If UN projections are correct, both trends are significant or likely in most

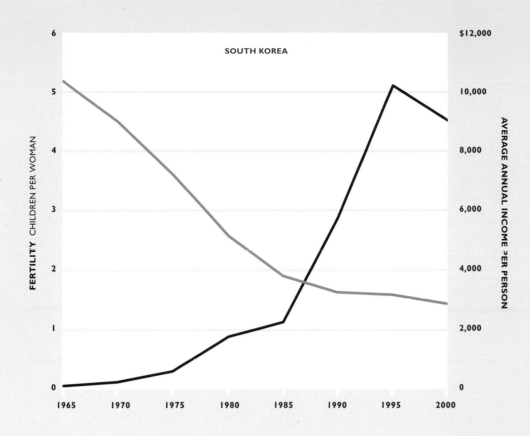

SOUTH KOREA

THAILAND

FIGURE 2.8 A AND B

THE ASIAN TIGER MODEL OF DEVELOPMENT, FROM 1965–2000

In several East and Southeast Asian countries, including South Korea and Thailand, declines in fertility largely preceded the period of rapid economic growth. In these countries, which economists refer to as the Asian Tigers, fertility decline may have helped prepare societies for economic change and democratization. Fertility is estimated by the total fertility rate, and income per person is estimated by gross national income per capita (World Bank Atlas Method, in 2001 US$). Downturns in average income between 1995 and 2000 are associated with the Asian currency crisis that began in 1996.

DATA SOURCES: UN POPULATION DIVISION, 2003, WORLD BANK, 2002

FERTILITY

INCOME

industrial countries. Still, the means by which an industrialized nation-state—one with an older, less densely populated society—is weakened and made vulnerable to civil or interstate conflict remain speculative and, as yet, untested by contemporary experience. Instead, the most logical hypothesis would be that older populations are, for several reasons developed subsequently in this report, less likely than younger ones to experience emerging civil conflict.

Demographic Dimensions of Conflict: Four Stress Factors and their Assessment

Having outlined the population changes that typically occur during demographic transition, it is time to return to the question posed previously: What early- and middle-transition forces might make states more vulnerable to civil conflict? The four chapters that follow focus on the factors that emerge from the current literature as the most immediate demographic stresses on the stability of nation-states in the various regions of the world:

- the political volatility of youthful population age structures;

- rapid urban population growth and the social turbulence it can promote;

- the challenges of declining availability, on a per capita basis, of cropland and fresh water; and

- the alarming death toll due to the proliferation of HIV/AIDS.

Each of these has been identified by a body of substantive research as a source of vulnerability to political instability, state failure or civil conflict. As in this chapter's previous analysis, there is no claim that these four demographic stress factors are causes of civil conflict, and none has shown itself to be insurmountable.

So, if some states have dealt with these challenges, why the concern? Most of the states facing these stresses lack the capacity to adequately respond. That is, they lack the financial systems and markets, adequate law enforcement and clearly delineated property rights, and the functioning educational and health care systems that are the foundations of strong states. And, in most cases, the level and quality of services that these countries have programmed—services including family planning, girls' education, maternal and child health, and HIV/AIDS prevention—that would help keep these demographic stress factors from worsening and becoming even greater challenges to governance in the future, are woefully inadequate.

Each of the next four chapters goes through an identical set of steps to arrive at its conclusions concerning these four demographic stress factors. Each begins with a review of destabilizing influences reported in relevant literature, and ends with an original quantitative analysis of the factor. For the purpose of the latter analysis, an appropriate demographic indicator was chosen to assess the strength of the stress factor in each country. The indicator's full range—from the country with the highest value to the lowest—was divided into four stress categories (extreme, high, medium, and low) using benchmarks drawn from relevant literature, or derived from available evidence or logical assumptions [see Appendix 2 for details on each factor]. To assess each factor and civil conflict during the period 1990 to 2000, countries were assigned to a stress category according to their indicator value in 1995. Data from the Conflict Data Project then were used to estimate, for each stress category, the *likelihood of an outbreak of a civil conflict*—calculated as the proportion of countries that experienced new outbreaks during the period. The four chapters feature a graph of this relationship, a world map showing countries coded for their 2005 level of demographic stress, and a discussion of these results (entitled "Risk Assessment").

The final chapter of the report (Chapter 7) identifies countries with a risk of civil conflict for the current decade, 2000 to 2010, based upon these same demographic factors. The chapter integrates 2005 data to arrive at a map and table highlighting countries presently experiencing multiple demographic risks.

Other Demographic Stress Factors: Migration and Shifts in Ethnic Composition

Researchers note that tensions between ethnic groups can arise when changes in *ethnic or religious composition* (the proportions of such groups in the population) are perceived as threats to the political character, traditions or cultural practices of one group or another. Tensions run especially high when such a demographic shift is led by an ethnic population—often a group in a high-growth stage of the demographic transition—that threatens to challenge numerically a politically powerful group.[43] These changes are difficult to quantify, as detailed ethnic data are unavailable from most countries (some, like Lebanon, suppress collection of these data to lessen tensions). Ethnic suspicions and fears often have been cultivated as a foundation for political organization and, on occasion, worked up into hatred and political violence.[44] Refugee movements and other cross-border migrations regularly evoke fears and anti-immigrant tensions in host countries.

Rapid, composition-altering migrations of politically powerful groups may represent the most direct demographic contributions to interethnic tensions. Throughout history, such migrations have foreshadowed the alteration or elimination of local institutions, cultural traditions and patterns of land use and control, producing some of today's most volatile fault lines of ethnic confrontation. Among the examples of this are Han settlements in western China, European and *mestizo* farmers abutting native communities throughout the Americas, Israeli settlements on the West Bank, Javanese on Indonesia's outer islands, and North Indians and Bengalis in the Tibeto-Burmese-speaking regions of eastern India.

Slower, more predictable shifts in ethnic composition also can play an influential role in the emergence of political tensions. Current demographic trends in Lebanon, Israel, Estonia and Fiji indicate future changes in ethnic or religious composition that, if continued, could precipitate constitutional crises or even civil violence.[45] And for larger countries with populous and growing regional ethnicities, the rise of ethnic separatism remains a perpetual possibility.

Despite a consensus that the relative sizes and distributions of ethnic populations in a country are important, political scientists are deeply divided as to what measures of ethnic populations reflect risks of state failure or civil conflict.[46] And because this theoretical uncertainty is exacerbated by a lack of data, differential population growth among ethnic and religious groups, and flows of refugees and other migrants were not included in our analyses. In a world that, in the last 50 years, has experienced unprecedented population growth, a four-fold growth in independent states and vastly uneven economic growth between them—and where the vast majority of national boundaries were drawn by conquerors and colonial administrators rather than through democratic processes—immigration and ethnic population shifts are bound to remain sources of political stress. And policies

TENSIONS BETWEEN ETHNIC GROUPS CAN ARISE WHEN CHANGES IN ETHNIC OR RELIGIOUS COMPOSITION ARE PERCEIVED AS THREATS TO THE POLITICAL CHARACTER, TRADITIONS OR CULTURAL PRACTICES OF ONE GROUP OR ANOTHER.

and trends that influence migration, ethnic relations, separatism and assimilation warrant intense study and the collection of more accurate data.

Finishing the Transition

Since the early 1960s, fertility in the world's developing countries has declined on average by half, and infant mortality by two-thirds. Population growth rates in these countries are down by more than half. These trends are currently among the most hopeful of all that influence social and economic development and political stability in some of the poorest countries. The lion's share of the credit for this transformation goes to those developing countries that have invested in improving access to family planning, maternal and child health care and other reproductive health services, and have followed through on policies that brought more girls into classrooms and more women into workplaces. These policies bolstered women's status and income, indirectly improved child nutrition, increased child survival, and expanded demand for modern contraception.

The states of the industrialized world can share credit in these achievements. A handful of donor countries, including the United States, the Scandinavian countries, the Netherlands and Japan, have provided critical financing, training, expertise and leadership, either through their own programs or through the United Nations Population Fund.[47]

Support for international family planning efforts has waned, however, in recent years—and at an inopportune time.[48] The need for more and better quality reproductive health care, contraceptives and counseling is growing. Nearly 1.1 billion young people aged 15 to 19 are entering their reproductive years, most of them unaware of the risks and responsibilities of sex and reproduction. Three million people die each year from AIDS. And still, around 515,000 women perish annually from largely preventable pregnancy-related causes, including about 70,000 deaths from unsafe abortions.[49]

Can the world change course? According to demographers, it already has. Growth of global population is decelerating more dramatically than was anticipated even in the mid-1990s. The United Nations Population Division, the most widely consulted demographic accountant on these matters, has set its 2002 medium variant projection—the one the division deems most predictive—at 7.9 billion people in 2025. That's about 1.5 billion more people than today. But it is also nearly 600 million *fewer* than the same UN demographers had projected for 2025 just a decade earlier.[50] Yet, the growth rate of population would be slower still if not for the fact that an estimated 38 percent of all pregnancies worldwide—some 80 million annually—are either unintended at the time or unwanted at any time.[51]

The global demographic transition is still far from complete. While one-third of the world's countries have made their way fully through the transition, more than a third remains in the early and middle phases. The future could see a continuation of today's impressive declines in fertility and childhood mortality, and a reversal in the HIV/AIDS pandemic—but only if policymakers support and fund the policies and programs that make such change possible. If the relationships between the demographic transition and conflict seen in the post-Cold War years hold in the coming decades, decisions made today that affect funding that facilitates this momentous transition could have an enormous influence, not only on demographic prospects, but also on the future of global security.

■ **KEY POINT** Demographic transition is the transformation of a population from conditions of short life expectancy and large families to long life expectancy and small families. About one-third of the world's countries—those with the longest histories of access to life-saving technologies and effective contraception—are in the last stage of this transition. At least another third of the world's countries, however, are still in the early and middle phases of the transition, in which death rates are low compared to historic levels, but birth rates remain relatively high. Such countries typically experience large proportions of young people and rapid population growth.

■ **KEY POINT** Analysis of data on population and newly initiated conflicts from 1990 to 2000 indicates that progress through the demographic transition—declines in birth rates and infant mortality rates—was associated with a consistent decline in the risk of civil conflict. A decline in the annual birth rate of five births per thousand people corresponded to a decline of just over 5 percent in the likelihood of civil conflict.

■ **KEY POINT** Population age structure has important implications. Some developing countries in the middle and late phases of the demographic transition experience a window of opportunity to exploit a *demographic bonus*—a large working-age population relative to proportionally smaller populations of dependent children and older people. The post-transition phase that many industrialized countries have entered typically leads to *population aging* and eventual population decline, absent offsetting migration. Such conditions are likely to challenge retirement systems and labor markets, but the influences of population aging on the civil and political order remain speculative and arguably helps dampen the likelihood of conflict.

■ **POLICY PRESCRIPTION** In recent decades the world as a whole has moved fairly rapidly through the early and middle stages of the demographic transition. Average family size is now a bit more than half of what it was in the early 1960s, and infant mortality has declined by two-thirds. Policies and investments that improved family planning and related reproductive health services and brought more girls into the classroom and women into the workplace are major reasons for this progress. Waning international support for family planning services, however, renders uncertain the pace of further progress through the transition.

BRIEFING POINTS Demographic Transition

CHAPTER THREE

Stress Factor One: The Youth Bulge

Demographically, the world is getting older but is still relatively young. A majority of the world's people are 27 years old or younger. Viewed from countries where most *young adults* (defined in this report as aged 15 to 29 years) have been educated or technically trained, and where their energy and ingenuity are sought by employers, such a large proportion of young people—a side effect of past population growth called the *youth bulge*—is seen as an asset. In fact, in economies where their numbers, productivity, savings and taxes support smaller subpopulations of children and elderly, economists have recognized that a large proportion of young workers provides a "demographic bonus" to economic growth (see Chapter Two: Transition's Opportunities).

In many other countries, however, the predominance of young adults constitutes a social challenge and a political hazard. This is particularly the case when employment opportunities are scarce and large numbers of young men feel frustrated in their search for status and livelihood. The evidence that a large proportion of young people is associated with the outbreak of political violence and warfare is among the best documented in the literature on population and conflict.

Age Structure and Its Dynamics

A youth bulge is a characteristic of the distinctive pyramid shape that appears when age groups in a rapidly growing population are illustrated in graphic form. In such a configuration—referred to as a *population pyramid*—each five-year age cohort, divided into male and female, is stacked atop the one just younger, with the tally of newborns to four-year olds at the base and number of the very old (aged 100 years and older) at the summit [Figure 3.1]. In this study, we follow the convention

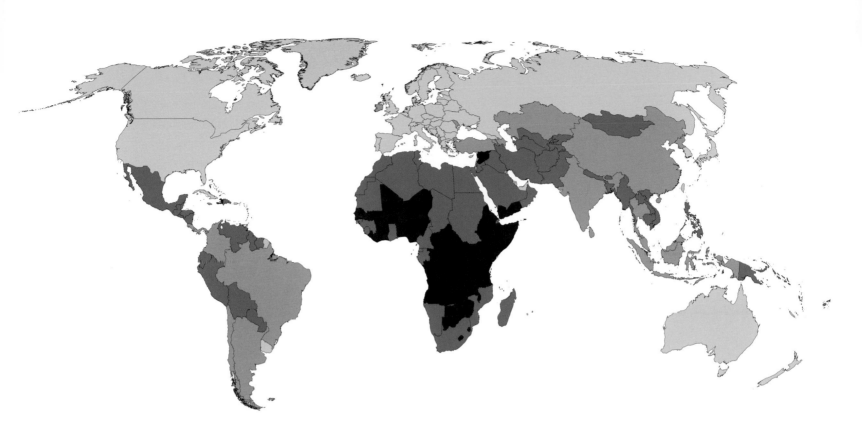

of other conflict researchers [Appendix 2F] who have assumed that a youth bulge has reached a significantly large proportion when young adults, aged 15 to 29 years, comprise more than 40 percent of all adults (those 15 and older). Countries whose young adult population is above 40 percent are typically in the early or middle phases of the demographic transition. In comparison, young adults currently comprise about 25 percent of all adults in the industrialized countries of North America and Europe.

At present, a large proportion of young adults results from one or more of several distinct demographic phenomena:

■ In populations in the early phase of the demographic transition, where consistent high fertility has been coupled with gradually declining rates of childhood mortality;

■ In populations in which HIV prevalence is high and AIDS is a major cause of premature adult death;

■ More rarely, in populations in which large numbers of adults emigrate and do not return; or

■ In middle-transition populations and even a few late-transition populations where the youth bulge, left over from high fertility in the past, lingers until smaller cohorts of children mature and reduce its proportion.

As noted, this last demographic phenomenon is transient. Once the smaller cohorts of young children born during the fertility decline enter their late teens, the proportional size of a youth bulge tends to shrink rapidly. Thailand's fertility began to decline around 1970, for example, and between 1990 and 1995 its population reached a total fertility rate just above two children per woman,

MAP 3

YOUNG ADULTS, 2005

Young Adults (aged 15–29 years) as a Proportion of All Adults (aged 15 and older)

DEMOGRAPHIC STRESS CATEGORY

▉ EXTREME: 50% OR MORE

▉ HIGH: 40% TO LESS THAN 50%

▉ MEDIUM: 30% TO LESS THAN 40%

▢ LOW: LESS THAN 30%

▢ NO DATA

DATA SOURCE: UNITED NATIONS POPULATION DIVISION, 2003

roughly the same level reported for the United States.[52] Between 1985 and 2000, Thailand's proportion of young adults dropped from 49 to 39 percent of all adults—still relatively high when compared to post-transition populations.

Thailand's experience with its youth bulge has been complex. Educated and industrious, the country's young workers (and particularly young women) have been a critical factor in the growth of its dynamic manufacturing and financial sectors. Simultaneously, youths have represented the most politically volatile segment of Thai society. Thailand's last experiences with mass anti-government demonstrations—which took the form of student and worker rioting that led to democratic reforms—occurred in the early 1980s, when the country's economy was challenged to absorb large numbers of young adults. Japan, South Korea and Sri Lanka experienced similarly rapid declines in the proportion of young adults in their populations as these countries progressed through their own demographic transitions. In each case, analysts have noted an association between high proportions of youth and a rise in civil unrest, state repression or state militancy [Figure 3.2].[53]

The Trouble with Men

Why are youth bulges so often volatile? The short answer is: too many young men with not enough to do. When a population as a whole is growing, ever larger numbers of young males come of age each year, ready for work, in search of respect from their male peers and elders. Typically, they are eager to achieve an identity, assert their independence and impress young females. While unemployment rates tend to be high in developing countries, unemployment among young adult males is usually from three to five times as high as adult rates, with lengthy periods between the end of schooling and first placement in a job.[54]

Are young males more prone to violence than older men, or than women? The preponderance of social research suggests that they are. Men account for about 90 percent of arrests for homicide in almost all countries surveyed.[55] All over the world, young men (in this case, defined as aged 15 to 34) are responsible for more than three-quarters of violent crimes.[56]

Youth and Warfare

A wealth of historical studies indicates that cycles of rebellion and military campaigns in the early-modern and modern world tended to coincide with periods when young adults comprised an unusually large proportion of the population. There are several variations to this hypothesis.

In the late-1960s, historian Herbert Moller observed that unusually chaotic periods in modern European history often followed several decades of rapid population growth. Moller hypothesized that the surge of young men entering adulthood contributed to under-employment, low wages, social discontent, and in some states, cycles of rebellion and repression. The wealthiest states enlisted the glut of restive young men into their armies, and then employed them at low wages and great danger to wrest territory from their continental neighbors and build overseas empires.[57]

Civil-conflict historian Jack Goldstone has argued that a bulge in the population of elite young adults was potentially the most destabilizing factor. Rebellions and religious movements of the 16th and 17th centuries were led by young men of the ruling class who, arriving at adulthood among an overly large cohort, found that their state's patronage system could not afford to reward them with

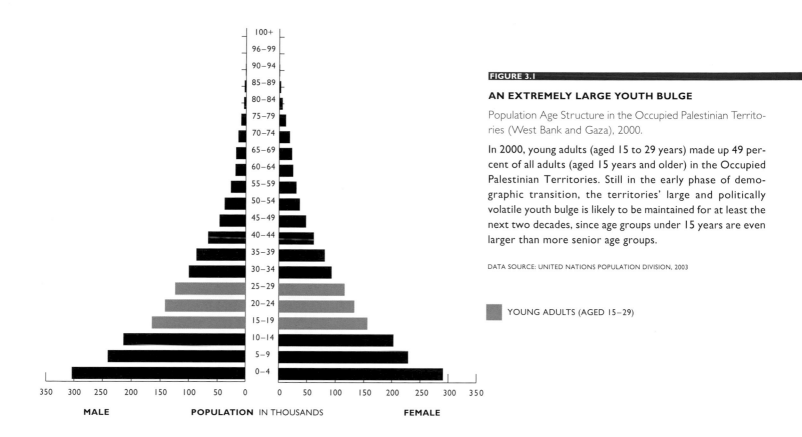

FIGURE 3.1

AN EXTREMELY LARGE YOUTH BULGE

Population Age Structure in the Occupied Palestinian Territories (West Bank and Gaza), 2000.

In 2000, young adults (aged 15 to 29 years) made up 49 percent of all adults (aged 15 years and older) in the Occupied Palestinian Territories. Still in the early phase of demographic transition, the territories' large and politically volatile youth bulge is likely to be maintained for at least the next two decades, since age groups under 15 years are even larger than more senior age groups.

DATA SOURCE: UNITED NATIONS POPULATION DIVISION, 2003

◼ YOUNG ADULTS (AGED 15–29)

the royal salary, land or bureaucratic position commensurate to their class and educational achievements.[58] The rising nation-states of Europe and the fading empires of Asia were left most vulnerable to civil conflict when the rapid enlargement of young adult populations coincided with economic downturn and urban growth. Rather than allow political discontent to fester, European militarists and Ottoman expansionists inducted thousands of young men of privilege, putting them in charge of literally millions of unschooled from the urban and rural under-classes, to serve their interests in military campaigns and overseas colonial exploits.

Studies of more recent conflicts come to similar conclusions. Christian Mesquida and Neil Weiner, political scientists at Canada's University of York who focused on the latter half of the 20th century, have shown that youth-laden populations in conflict-torn regions—such as the Balkans and Central Asia—are more likely to experience highly intense conflicts (measured in battle-related deaths per thousand people) than less youthful populations.[59] Other researchers have reported that countries with high proportions of youth also have a high likelihood of becoming embroiled in civil conflicts.[60] Drawing on case studies of several Asian countries, political scientist Gary Fuller at the University of Hawaii warns that rapidly industrializing cities and frontier areas can offer a spawning ground for political unrest because thousands of young men migrate to these sites in search of livelihood.[61]

Women's status in society may also affect the vulnerability to conflict that a large youth bulge presents. Political scientists increasingly report evidence from case studies and historical accounts that suggest the political volatility of men is exacerbated by the social and political exclusion of women, who, surveys show, are relatively averse to the use of force to resolve civil and interstate disputes.[62]

THE YOUTH BULGE AND ITS ASSOCIATION WITH MILITARISM AND POLITICAL INSTABILITY

Comparing Japan, South Korea, Thailand and Sri Lanka.

Recent history suggests some intriguing associations between periods of large proportions of young adults (aged 15–29, as a proportion of all adults, aged 15 and older) and periods of social unrest, militarism, civil conflict and even international aggression. In East Asia some of this disorder led to democratic reforms. In other cases, under-employed young men were swept up into militant ethnic and political movements, and in the case of Japan, into interstate warfare. Some countries, however, have been able to reduce the political risks associated with a large youth bulge through job creation, land redistribution or by sending young adults to work overseas. Each graph shows a downward trend in the total fertility rate, which typically precedes a decline in the proportion of young adults.

DATA SOURCES: UN POPULATION DIVISION, 2003; G. FULLER, 1995; N. OGAWA, 2002

FIGURE 3.2A

JAPAN

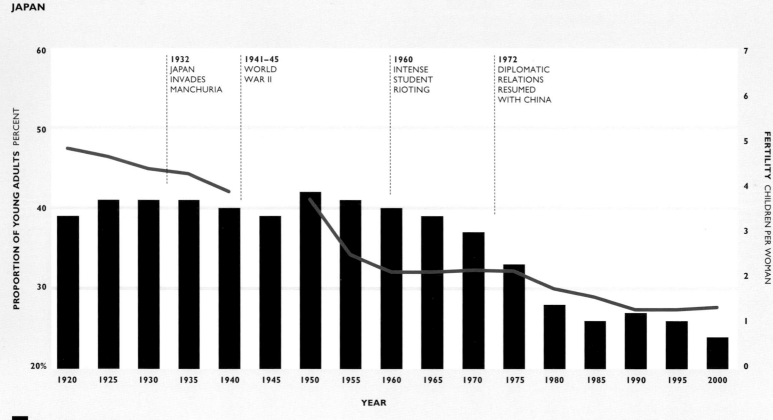

1932
JAPAN
INVADES
MANCHURIA

1941–45
WORLD
WAR II

1960
INTENSE
STUDENT
RIOTING

1972
DIPLOMATIC
RELATIONS
RESUMED
WITH CHINA

■ PROPORTION OF YOUNG ADULTS

▬ FERTILITY

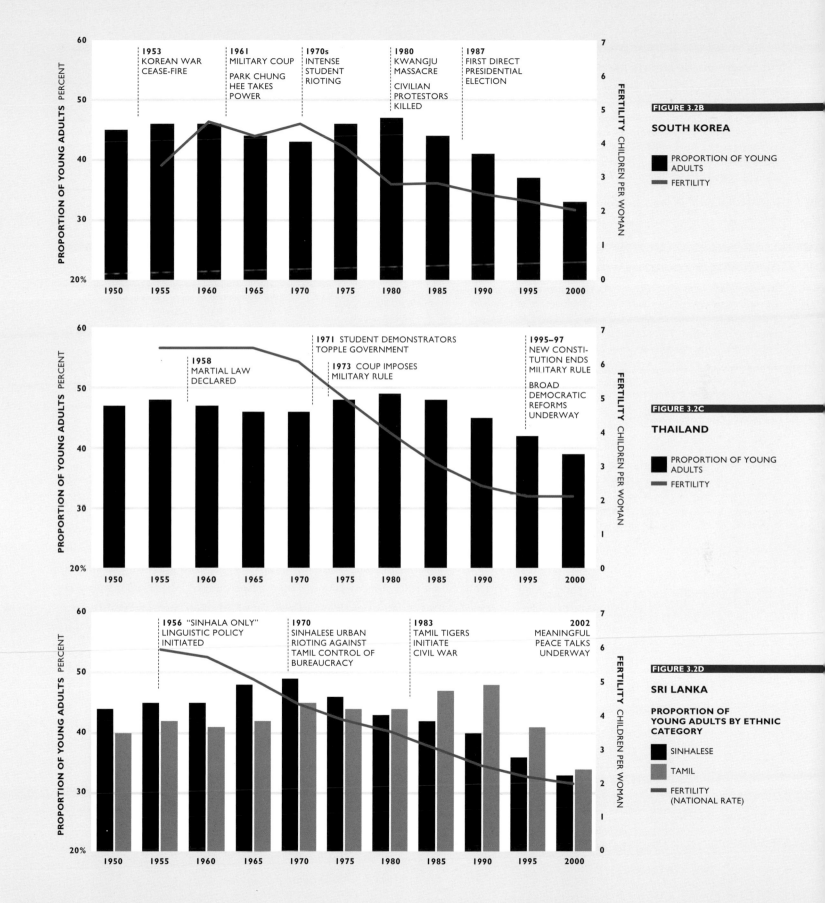

FIGURE 3.2B

SOUTH KOREA

■ PROPORTION OF YOUNG ADULTS

— FERTILITY

1953 KOREAN WAR CEASE-FIRE

1961 MILITARY COUP

PARK CHUNG HEE TAKES POWER

1970s INTENSE STUDENT RIOTING

1980 KWANGJU MASSACRE

CIVILIAN PROTESTORS KILLED

1987 FIRST DIRECT PRESIDENTIAL ELECTION

FIGURE 3.2C

THAILAND

■ PROPORTION OF YOUNG ADULTS

— FERTILITY

1958 MARTIAL LAW DECLARED

1971 STUDENT DEMONSTRATORS TOPPLE GOVERNMENT

1973 COUP IMPOSES MILITARY RULE

1995–97 NEW CONSTITUTION ENDS MILITARY RULE

BROAD DEMOCRATIC REFORMS UNDERWAY

FIGURE 3.2D

SRI LANKA

PROPORTION OF YOUNG ADULTS BY ETHNIC CATEGORY

■ SINHALESE

■ TAMIL

— FERTILITY (NATIONAL RATE)

1956 "SINHALA ONLY" LINGUISTIC POLICY INITIATED

1970 SINHALESE URBAN RIOTING AGAINST TAMIL CONTROL OF BUREAUCRACY

1983 TAMIL TIGERS INITIATE CIVIL WAR

2002 MEANINGFUL PEACE TALKS UNDERWAY

PROPORTION OF YOUNG ADULTS PERCENT

FERTILITY CHILDREN PER WOMAN

TABLE 3.1

THE YOUTH BULGE AND ITS ASSOCIATION WITH CIVIL CONFLICT, 1990–2000

Countries with more than 40 percent of young adults (aged 15 to 29 years) in the population of adults (aged 15 and older) were 2.3 times as likely to experience an outbreak of civil conflict as countries with smaller proportions during the 1990s. The likelihood of conflict was calculated as the proportion of countries in a category that experienced a newly initiated civil conflict, from 1990 to 2000. Data comprises values from 145 countries, which excludes conflicts that persisted or reemerged from the late 1980s. Data enumerating population by age were from 1995.

Demographic Stress Category	Proportion of Young Adults 1995	Likelihood of an Outbreak of Civil Conflict 1990–2000
Extreme and High	40.0% and greater	33%
Medium	30.0 to 39.9%	18%
Low	less than 30.0%	11%

DATA SOURCES: UN POPULATION DIVISION, 2003; WALLENSTEEN AND SOLLENBERG, 2000; GLEDITSCH ET AL., 2002

TABLE 3.2

THE NUMBER OF COUNTRIES WITH A LARGE YOUTH BULGE, 1975–2005

Because of high rates of fertility in the past, populations in the majority of the world's countries still experience large youth bulges. The number of countries with more than 40 percent of all adults (aged 15 years and older) as young adults (aged 15 to 29 years) has declined markedly since 1990. At the same time, however, the subset of these countries, where proportions of young adults are over 50 percent, has grown. This latter, most-extreme category principally comprises countries that have sustained high fertility while infant mortality has declined. Currently, almost all of the countries with a population of young adults at a proportion higher than 50 percent are in sub-Saharan Africa and the Middle East.

Year	Number of Countries	
	Proportion of young adults in adult population:	
	40% and greater	50% and greater
1975	121	17
1985	117	32
1995	103	28
2005	95	37

DATA SOURCE: UN POPULATION DIVISION, 2003

Risk Assessment: The Youth Bulge

While there is substantial evidence in the literature of a large youth bulge's capacity to stress a political system, testing the relationship using demographic and conflict data from the 1990s provided a quantitative indication of the level of risk associated with this factor. Using age composition data from 1995, countries were placed in one of four demographic stress categories according to the size of their youth bulge: where young adults comprised more than 50 percent of adults, countries were assumed to experience *extreme stress* conditions; from 40 percent of adults to just less than 50 percent, *high stress*; from 30 percent to less than 40 percent, *medium stress*; less than 30 percent, *low stress* [for additional information on these categories, see Appendix 2H]. The likelihood of civil conflict in each category was calculated as the percentage of countries that experienced civil conflict from 1990 to 2000 (excluding countries with persistent or recurring conflict).

Did a large youth bulge appear to impart risk of civil conflict during the 1990s? Our analysis suggests that it did—roughly half of all high and extreme risk states (where young adults comprised 40 percent or more of all adults) experienced civil conflict sometime from 1990 to 2000 [Table 3.1], 2.3 times the likelihood of countries below that benchmark.

As fertility declines around the globe, large youth bulges should dissipate. But trends in the youth bulge reveal a growing bifurcation between two sets of developing countries: those well along in the demographic transition, and countries in the early phase of the transition. Between 1990 and 2000, the numbers of states with high proportions of young adults (40 percent or more of all adults) decreased by about one-sixth, no doubt in large part because fertility was falling in East Asia, the Caribbean and Latin America. Simultaneously, a group of early-transition countries—mostly in sub-Saharan Africa, the Middle East and South and Central Asia—experienced rapid growth in the age-15-to-29 portion of their populations, to levels exceeding 50 percent of all adults [Table 3.2]. The toll of adult deaths due to AIDS threatens to increase the relative size of the youth bulge among populations with high HIV prevalence, which could prolong this trend. [See Chapter 6, on the demographic impacts of HIV/AIDS.]

Our analysis of current patterns of age structure considers the year 2005, a future so close that population projections can be used with confidence [Map 3]. The United Nations projects that young adults will make up 40 percent of adults or more in just over 100 countries that year; in 38 countries they will account for more than half. Of these extremely youthful countries, 31 (comprising 82 percent of the country total) are in sub-Saharan Africa, two are in the Middle East (Yemen and Syria), and three in Central America and the Caribbean (Haiti, Guatemala and Nicaragua).

In the short term, governments can remedy a portion of the risk associated with jobless youth by investing in job creation and training, and by promoting entrepreneurship among them.[63] In the longer term, governments can facilitate fertility decline by supporting policies that promote access to family planning services—including reproductive health services and accurate information for young adults—and by increasing girls' educational attainment and women's opportunities for employment outside the home. For countries in the early stages of the demographic transition, it could take nearly two decades after fertility begins to fall to observe a significant reduction in the proportion of young adults. But given the many risks of delaying the demographic transition, this only underscores the need for governments to put supportive policies into effect sooner rather than later.

■ KEY POINT Countries in which young adults made up a large proportion of the adult population—40 percent or more—were more than twice as likely to experience an outbreak of civil conflict during the 1990s as those below this benchmark. These youth-bulge countries are in the developing world, where youth unemployment rates are generally three to five times that of adults.

■ KEY POINT High fertility rates coupled with declining infant mortality are the major reason for high proportions of young adults. In East Asia, proportions of young adults began to decline significantly less than two decades after fertility began its own fall.

■ POLICY PRESCRIPTION To deal with chronic unemployment of young adults in the short term, governments should invest in training and job creation, and promote entrepreneurship among youth. But necessary long-term changes in age structure in early-transition countries occur through fertility decline. Countries have promoted this change by supporting access to voluntary family planning services, increasing girls' educational achievement, and promoting women's access to economic opportunity. And, in a world where AIDS is a major cause of illness and premature death—with demographic impacts that threaten to expand already large youth bulges in some countries—governments should promote full access to reproductive health services and accurate information to young adults.

BRIEFING POINTS Youth

CHAPTER FOUR

Stress Factor Two:
Rapid Urban Growth

Urbanization—technically, the proportional growth of urban dwellers in any population at the expense of the rural proportion—appears to be an inexorable historical trend. The movement to cities has contributed to economic growth and globalization, as increasing numbers of people find homes close to schools, health clinics, workplaces and communication networks that connect them to the rest of the world. The character of urbanization is nonetheless changing as the biggest cities in the developing world gain denser populations and extend further into the countryside, and as crossroads and market towns rapidly transform into urban centers.[64]

Once, industrialized countries claimed nearly all the world's biggest cities. Today, only four of the 20 cities with more than 10 million residents (dubbed *megacities* by demographers) are in the industrial world. Developing-country urban populations grew from about 300 million in 1950 (then 18 percent of these countries' total populations) to more than 2 billion (and 40 percent of total developing-country populations) today. The vast majority of urban population growth now occurs in the developing world [Figure 4.1]. Three out of every four Latin Americans are urban dwellers, a proportion on par with the industrialized world. In the two most rapidly urbanizing regions, Africa and Asia, four of every 10 people live in urban areas. And while about half of Asia's urban growth still lies ahead, its current urban population is already larger than the entire population of all industrialized countries combined.[65]

The remarkable rates of growth that some urban centers in the developing world sustained during the 1970s and 1980s—several doubled in size in less than a decade—could not help but flood job markets, exacerbate inter-ethnic competition, challenge the adequacy of existing services and

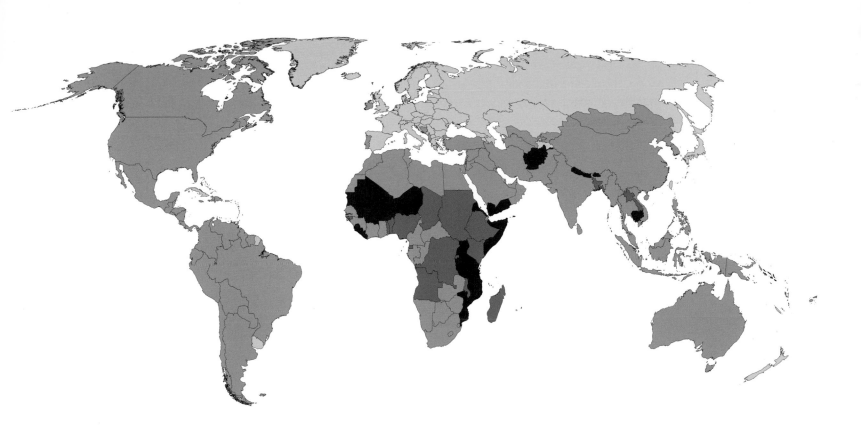

infrastructure, and deplete city budgets. Municipal governments in the least developed countries were the least capable of mustering the human and financial resources to contend with these problems, especially when the poorest, non-taxable segment of the urban population continued growing rapidly.[66] More than rural discord, that of urban areas has drawn from diverse social classes. Among the recruits are politicized students, the angry unemployed, and the politically disaffected. Many of these, especially those from middle-class backgrounds, bring with them the skills and resources to organize and finance civil protest.[67]

The Good, the Bad and the Urban

Urbanization is, by and large, a progressive demographic trend. Cities are centers of industry and education. Their populations are almost always ahead of those in rural areas in gaining access to new technologies, information and goods. Because health care delivery in cities is much more cost-effective than in the countryside, governments prioritize urban clinics, and urban dwellers are almost invariably the first to experience the declines in infant mortality and fertility that lead to the demographic transition. Recent declines in fertility in Africa, for example, are mostly an urban phenomenon, with far less change in childbearing behavior in rural areas.[68]

Cities possess other demographically remarkable traits. Because they attract young workers and students, urban areas often have significant youth bulges.[69] Urban populations also tend to be diverse, bringing disparate ethnic, religious and regional groups into close social contact. Such interaction can have positive social implications when local governments and community leaders have

MAP 4

URBAN GROWTH, 2000–05

Average Annual Rate
of Change of the Urban
Population

**DEMOGRAPHIC STRESS
CATEGORY**

EXTREME: 5% OR MORE

HIGH: 4%
TO LESS THAN 5%

MEDIUM: 1%
TO LESS THAN 4%

LOW: LESS THAN 1%

NO DATA

DATA SOURCE: UNITED NATIONS
POPULATION DIVISION, 2002

the will and resources to overcome differences. Very often, however, cities are where these communities engage most intensely in economic and political competition, and where historic grievances and cultural misunderstandings are likely to surface. Urban housing and job markets tend to illuminate disparities in access to education, capital and political power. For centuries the site of criminal activity, social protest, and labor unrest, urban areas—particularly those in Asia—are increasingly the principal locus of ethnic and religious conflict.[70]

A 1992 incident in India reflects the urban influence on conflict. Outside the normally sleepy, rural northern town of Ayodhya, a crowd of some 150,000 Hindu militants descended upon a virtually abandoned 16th-century mosque, believing it to sit on the site of the birthplace of Rama, an important Hindu deity. The militants attacked security forces and onlookers and destroyed the mosque. The violence, however, did not spread through the nearby rural countryside, where Muslim and Hindu communities coexisted peaceably. Instead, the hatred returned hundreds of kilometers by bus and by rail to its origins in the growing Indian cities of Mumbai (Bombay), Calcutta, Ahmedabad and Delhi. Nearly 95 percent of the 1,500 lives lost in communal riots triggered by this incident were those of urban dwellers.[71] In March of 2002, more than 850 people died and thousands lost their homes in three days of rioting in Ahmedabad and nearby Vadodara. These incidents, some of which were reported to have been condoned by local government leaders, unraveled efforts by moderates to broker cooperation between Indian Muslim and Hindu politicians and aggravated already delicate relations between India and neighboring Pakistan.[72]

Growing Pains

Since 1950, the world's urban population has climbed from about 750 million to just under 3 billion today. Some 60 percent of current urban population growth is, on average, the result of *natural increase*—urban births minus deaths. Rural-to-urban migration accounts for nearly all of the urban growth that remains, with the exception of relatively small annual contributions from *reclassification* (a change in the designation of rural land to urban land).[73]

What drives the unrelenting wave of migration that has vastly accelerated world urbanization? Economists describe the phenomenon as the net result of the "push" from stagnating rural areas and the "pull" of more promising urban economic and social conditions. Case studies suggest that most rural-to-urban migrants in Asia and Latin America are lured to cities by better job prospects and the attractions of modernization.[74] In sub-Saharan Africa, where urban economic opportunities are limited, migrants relocate to escape recurrent drought, warfare, or the shortage of agricultural work.[75]

Demographers see the rapid growth of cities as an outgrowth of the demographic transition. Despite the potential opportunity in an urban economy and insecurity of rural subsistence living, analyses of data show that the rate of national population growth, by itself, explains most urban population growth, including rural-to-urban migration [Figure 4.2]. Although fertility rates are consistently lower in cities than in the countryside worldwide, the pace of urban population growth in most countries tends to remain about 50 percent more rapid than national rates as a whole, regardless of the region. If this pattern holds in the future, reductions in population growth rates would likely be repeated in urban areas.

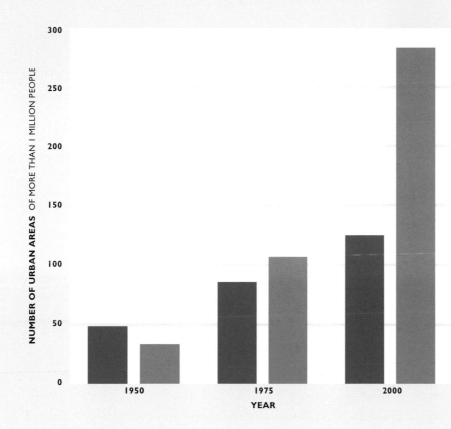

NUMBER OF URBAN AREAS OF MORE THAN 1 MILLION PEOPLE

300

250

200

150

100

50

0

1950   1975   2000

YEAR

FIGURE 4.1

GROWTH IN THE NUMBER OF LARGE CITIES IN THE DEVELOPED AND DEVELOPING COUNTRIES, 1950–2000

Urban areas with populations larger than 1 million more than quadrupled in the second half of the last century, from about 80 in 1950 to more than 400 today worldwide. Most of that expansion occurred in developing countries, in which a growing majority of the world's large cities are found.

DATA SOURCE: UN POPULATION DIVISION, 2002

■ IN DEVELOPED COUNTRIES

■ IN DEVELOPING COUNTRIES

FIGURE 4.2

THE RELATIONSHIP BETWEEN NATIONAL POPULA-TION GROWTH AND URBAN GROWTH, 1995–2000

Urban population growth averages about 1.5 times the rate of national population growth. This relationship holds fairly consistently worldwide, despite the fact that birthrates tend to be lower in cities than in surrounding rural areas. The strength of this relationship implies that the country-wide level of population growth is a principal factor in the migration-driven growth of urban populations, and it lends support to the conclusion that declining population growth rates tend to slow rural-to-urban migration and urban growth generally (see Appendix 3 for statistical re-lationship).

DATA SOURCES: UN POPULATION DIVISION, 2002, 2003

☐ EASTERN EUROPE AND FORMER SOVIET UNION

☐ WESTERN EUROPE AND OTHER INDUSTRIALIZED COUNTRIES

■ SUB-SAHARAN AFRICA

☐ MIDDLE EAST AND NORTH AFRICA

■ LATIN AMERICA AND CARIBBEAN

▬ ALL COUNTRIES (ON AVERAGE)

URBAN POPULATION GROWTH RATE PERCENT

8

6

4

2

0%

-2

0%   2   4   6

NATIONAL POPULATION GROWTH RATE PERCENT

Distributional patterns of urban growth are shifting within countries. Population growth is slowing in larger urban areas—those exceeding 5 million residents—while continuing apace in *secondary* urban areas, those with fewer people. This may be a reflection of the recent faltering progress of education and health care in large developing-country cities, or due perhaps to other emerging factors that discourage large-city growth or favor small cities.[76]

As the world shifts towards more cities and denser settlement, urban warfare is likely to play a greater role in military operations. For veterans of the U.S. intervention in Mogadishu, Somalia in 1993, Russian veterans of the battle over the Chechen capital of Grozny the following year, and American and British troops trying to maintain order in Iraqi cities as this is written, the prospect of more urban warfare is tactically challenging and psychologically unsettling. In these battles, the advantages of close air support, artillery and armor were often lost among the urban labyrinth of buildings, roadways and sewers. Alongside the elevated physical and psychological risks to military personnel, modern urban warfare has resulted in high rates of civilian casualties and streams of refugees.[77]

Risk Assessment: Rapid Urban Growth

Can a quantitative relationship be detected between rapid urban population growth and the likelihood of civil conflict? An analysis of the 1990s was used to address this question, employing the same methods used to determine levels of risk imparted by the youth bulge. Again, countries were divided among four demographic stress categories based on urban population growth rates for the period 1990–95. Where this growth rate was at 5 percent or greater, countries were assumed to experience *extreme stress* conditions; from 4 percent to just less than 5 percent, *high stress;* from 1 percent to less than 4 percent, *medium stress;* less than 1 percent, *low stress.* [For additional information, see Appendix 21.] The likelihood of civil conflict in each category was calculated as the percentage of countries that experienced civil conflict from 1990 to 2000 (excluding countries with persistent or recurring conflict).

TABLE 4.1

URBAN POPULATION GROWTH AND ITS ASSOCIATION WITH CIVIL CONFLICT, 1990–2000

Countries with urban population growth over 4 percent per year had twice the likelihood of experiencing an outbreak of civil conflict as countries with slower rates during the 1990s. The likelihood of conflict was calculated as the proportion of countries in a category that experienced a newly initiated civil conflict, from 1990 to 2000. Data comprises values from 145 countries, which excludes conflicts that persisted or reemerged from the late 1980s.

DATA SOURCES: UN POPULATION DIVISION, 2001; WALLENSTEEN AND SOLLENBERG, 2001; GLEDITSCH ET AL., 2002

Demographic Stress Category	Annual Rate of Urban Population Growth 1990–95	Likelihood of an Outbreak of Civil Conflict 1990–2000
Extreme and High	4.0% and greater	40%
Medium	1.0 to 3.9%	20%
Low	less than 1.0%	19%

Our analysis of the 1990s suggests that countries with high urban population growth rates—above 4 percent per year—were about twice as likely to experience civil conflict as those countries below that benchmark [Table 4.1]. While some of the strength of this relationship may stem from the role that urban areas play as catchments for refugees from rural civil conflicts, much of the developing world's urban growth is following a long-term trend. Barring unexpected demographic surprises, the vast majority of the world's population growth in the next 25 years will likely occur or end up in the cities and metropolises of Asia and sub-Saharan Africa—regions where urban population growth rates remain relatively high [Map 4].[78]

Urban population growth is a double-edged sword. The very features that allow some cities to fuel national progress and economic growth—youthful population, ethnic and religious diversity, a middle class and proximity to political power—are potential sources of volatility in others. This demographic indicator deserves more attention from analysts of conflict. And policymakers should strongly consider programs that strengthen urban governance, stimulate job creation, and foster ethnic-community relations in the short-term. Over the longer term, the slowing of population growth in most of the world's countries offers hope that the growth of cities, too, will slow to a more manageable pace.

■ **KEY POINT** Countries with rapid rates of urban population growth—4 percent per year or more—were about twice as likely as countries below this benchmark to experience civil conflict in the 1990s.

■ **KEY POINT** Factors that have made industrial-world cities prosperous—ethnic diversity, a middle class, and proximity to political power—are potential sources of volatility for many rapidly growing cities in the developing world. A high proportion of youth, a trait of many of these cities, adds another conflict risk factor to the rapid growth of urban areas.

■ **KEY POINT** Countries experiencing high rates of population growth generally experience rates of urban population growth about 50 percent higher than national population growth rates. Where population growth rates have slowed, in both developing and developed countries, urban growth rates have declined.

■ **POLICY PRESCRIPTION** Reviews of successful urban programs suggest that programs that improve the quality and capacity of urban governance, increase rates of job creation, and improve ethnic-community relations are likely to help reduce the risk of civil and ethnic violence. In early-transition countries, declines in national rates of population growth could help reduce risks by slowing the growth rates of urban population.

**BRIEFING POINTS
Urban Growth**

CHAPTER FIVE

Stress Factor Three: Competition for Cropland and Fresh Water

Dozens of states have already reached what are, by historical standards and by expert assessments of development needs, alarmingly low levels of cropland and available fresh water relative to their population. The most chronic per capita scarcities of *cropland* (land either cultivated, in permanent crops or in temporary fallow [Appendix 2J]) and *renewable fresh water* (supplies of fresh water refreshed by current precipitation, including rivers, lakes and shallow aquifers) occur in countries dominated by deserts or mountainous terrain and on islands. Many other countries, however, have come to these conditions through rapid population growth over the past half century or so [Table 5.1]— a dynamic that reflects at least partial progress through the demographic transition.

This trend does not alarm most economists. They note that most European and some Asian states—in recent years, South Korea, Taiwan and Japan—now rely on export industries to create urban jobs and bring in foreign exchange. And most of these countries have increased imports of food and animal feed to ease burgeoning agricultural demands on land and fresh water. Other countries have become more water-efficient; some have turned to desalinization as a means, albeit costly, to supplement sparse drinking-water; and in a few cases, water-short countries actually import fresh water via pipelines and by other direct means.[79] Many of the developing countries experiencing dwindling levels of cropland and renewable fresh water per person, however, show little immediate promise of attracting the capital needed to rapidly industrialize or radically transform their land and water use practices. And despite the broad global trends toward urbanization and mechanized large-scale agriculture, small-scale farming remains the major source of economic security in sub-Saharan Africa and southern Asia, and a sensitive root of tradition and cultural identity in the developing world.[80]

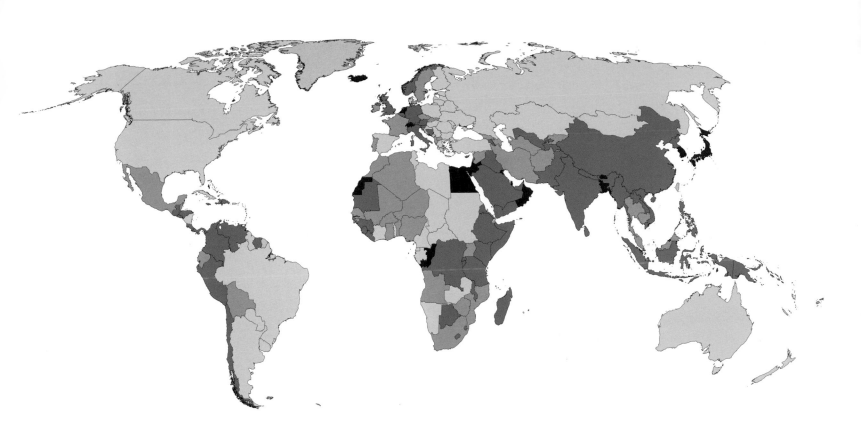

As environmental-conflict theorists Thomas Homer-Dixon and Miriam Lowi have separately concluded, civil disputes over cropland and fresh water have rarely, if ever, appeared as the simple product of population-driven scarcity alone.[81] Acute and potentially explosive threats to rural livelihoods—such as eviction from farmlands, loss of traditional access to natural resources, and impoverishment—typically have emerged in the context of a tangled web of historic inequities that collided with changes occurring in the local economic, ecological and political environments. In the recent past, these rapid changes have most often been induced by combinations of population growth, land degradation and government policies.

The literature review and data analysis presented here indicate that the relationship between cropland and freshwater per capita scarcities and the risk of civil conflict are, by themselves, weaker than the risks associated with the youth bulge and with rapid urban population growth. Why should that be? Arguably, answers lie in the abilities of industrial countries—which have already passed through the demographic transition—to mediate these scarcities with technology and trade. In terms of civil conflict, disputes over cropland appear to be generally more volatile than those that occur within countries over fresh water. This may relate to dissimilarities in the ways the two resources are owned, priced and accessed.

Readers may question why this chapter does not explore population-influenced natural resource disputes between nation-states, rather than simply within them. The research literature suggests that the resource-related tensions that have instigated minor armed hostilities between states in the recent past—disputes related to controls over transboundary water or ocean fishing rights, for example—

MAP 5.1

CROPLAND AVAILABILITY, 2005

DEMOGRAPHIC STRESS CATEGORY
CROPLAND IN HECTARES PER PERSON

- EXTREME: LESS THAN 0.07
- HIGH: 0.07 TO LESS THAN 0.21
- MEDIUM: 0.21 TO LESS THAN 0.35
- LOW: 0.35 OR MORE
- NO DATA

DATA SOURCES: UNITED NATIONS POPULATION DIVISION, 2003; FOOD AND AGRICULTURAL ORGANIZATION, 2002

TABLE 5.1

CROPLAND AND FRESHWATER SCARCITY, 1975–2025

Recent population growth has been responsible for the steady increase in the number of countries classified as experiencing scarcity in per capita availability of cropland, or in per capita availability of renewable fresh water. Simultaneously, substantial increases have occurred in the number of people estimated to be living in countries classified as land scarce or water scarce. According to the medium variant of the UN population projections for 2025, these trends are likely to continue for the foreseeable future in most regions of the developing world. In this report, countries that are classified as either cropland scarce or freshwater scarce — which are assessed by extremely conservative benchmarks (Appendix 2J) — comprise the extreme-demographic-stress category of this factor.

Year	Per Capita Cropland Scarcity		Per Capita Freshwater Scarcity	
	COUNTRIES	POPULATION	COUNTRIES	POPULATION
	Less than 0.07 hectares per person	in Millions	Less than 1,000 cubic meters per person	in Millions
1975	16	173	9	45
2000	20	425	15	245
2025	29	639	23	852

DATA SOURCES: UNITED NATIONS POPULATION DIVISION, 2003; WORLD RESOURCES INSTITUTE, 2003; FAO, 2002

have generally ended in non-violent outcomes such as negotiated agreements or the formation of regulatory institutions to resolve disputes.[82] Past outcomes are no guarantee of future security, however. The projected demographic futures of the Middle East, South Asia, Africa and Latin America look very different from the past. According to a recent study by researchers at the International Food Policy Research Institute, limited fresh water could impose serious constraints on food production increases in many developing countries within the next few decades.[83] The world's 261 international rivers and their watersheds account for about 60 percent of the world's freshwater supply.[84] And these transboundary water supplies are critical to agriculture as well as to growing numbers of household users in expanding urban areas, and to industrial development and employment.

Population and Rural Livelihood Insecurity

Population growth clearly plays a distinctive role in driving the subdivision of farmland and boosting the demand for urban and irrigation water. These processes have prompted governments to subsidize commercial farming, build large dams and underwrite frontier settlement schemes, driving migrants into indigenous reserves, to overburdened cities and across borders. These interventions, in turn, have exacerbated political tensions between ethnic groups, between indigenous groups and migrants, between local people and landowners of large holdings, between rural and urban dwellers, and between farmers and the state. And they have reduced the set of available solutions. With only a handful of scattered exceptions, the last half-century of rapid population growth has virtually eliminated the political "safety valves" of frontier settlement,[85] irrigation-assisted agricultural expansion, and rural land reform.

Several cases in which local land and water disputes mushroomed into larger threats are well documented. The Zapatista rebellion in southern Mexico grew out of centuries-old tensions between land-poor peasants and politically connected local elites. Hemmed in by other poor settlers and excluded from government-protected forest reserves, Mayans in the state of Chiapas organized an insurgency geared to lay claim to lands deeded to large landowners—a group that was locally politically powerful, but upon whom most Mexicans looked unfavorably. The scale and organization of

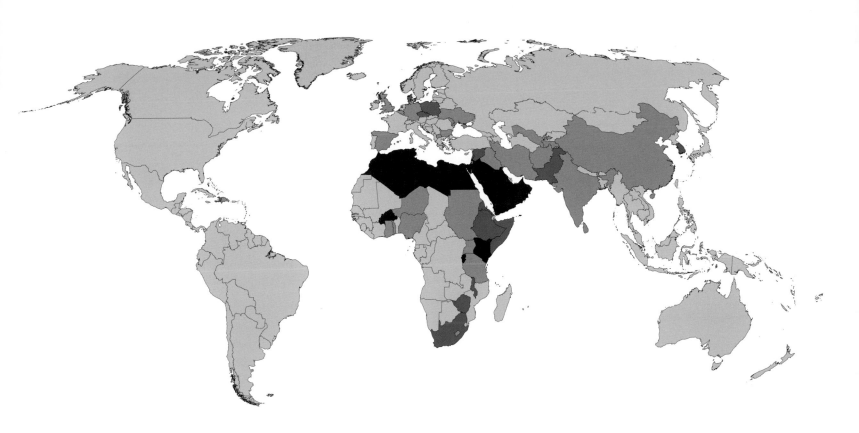

MAP 5.2

**FRESHWATER
AVAILABILITY, 2005**

**DEMOGRAPHIC STRESS
CATEGORY**
RENEWABLE FRESHWATER
IN CUBIC METERS PER PERSON

◼ EXTREME: LESS THAN 1,000

◼ HIGH: 1,000
TO LESS THAN 1,667

◼ MEDIUM: 1,667
TO LESS THAN 3,000

◻ LOW: 3,000 OR MORE

◻ NO DATA

DATA SOURCES: UNITED NATIONS
POPULATION DIVISION, 2003: WORLD
RESOURCES INSTITUTE, 2003

the Zapatista rebellion unnerved foreign investors and may have contributed to the nation-wide monetary crisis that eventually undermined the power of the ruling regime.[86]

In another case, water scarcity in the Middle East aggravates ethnic animosities and could complicate future efforts to resolve the region's longstanding conflict. In the Occupied West Bank, Israel has restricted Arabs from drilling new wells for agricultural purposes for more than three decades. Israeli settlers have continued to drill deeper, in some cases leading water tables to drop below levels at which Palestinian wells can reach them. Since 1967, the proportion of their cropland that Palestinian farmers irrigate has dropped from 27 percent to around 5 percent, adding to unemployment and productivity loss, as well as to the list of grievances against Israeli rule.[87]

In several cases, weak governments have supported the violent actions of land-poor groups to undermine their regime's political rivals. During the mid-1990s, politicians from the ruling party in Kenya encouraged ethnic Kalenjins in the Rift Valley to perpetuate violence to recoup land lost in the decades following independence to farmers from larger and wealthier ethnic groups who opposed the regime.[88] States have used people with land-related grievances to oppose or depose European farmers in Zimbabwe and Tutsis in Rwanda and Burundi.[89]

Risk Assessment: Population Growth, Cropland and Fresh Water

Were populations that experienced low levels of either cropland or fresh water, on a per capita basis, more prone to civil conflict than other states during the 1990s? To determine if this was the case, countries were assigned (as in previous chapters) to four demographic stress categories, based upon

TABLE 5.2

CROPLAND AND FRESHWATER AVAILABILITY AND THEIR ASSOCIATION WITH CIVIL CONFLICT, 1990–2000

Countries with either low per capita levels of cropland or fresh water were 1.5 times as likely to experience an outbreak of civil conflict as countries with more adequate supplies during the 1990s. Data comprises values from 144 countries, which excludes conflicts that persisted or reemerged from the late 1980s. Population data are 1995 estimates.

DATA SOURCES: UN POPULATION DIVISION, 2003; WORLD RESOURCES INSTITUTE, 2000; FAO, 2002; WALLENSTEEN AND SOLLENBERG, 2001; GLEDITSCH ET AL., 2002.

Demographic Stress Category	Cropland 1995	Renewable Fresh Water 1995	Likelihood of an Outbreak of Civil Conflict 1990–2000
	hectares per person	cubic meters per person	
Extreme/High	Less than 0.21	Less than 1,667	30%
Medium	0.21 to less than 0.35	1,667 to less than 3,000	29%
Low	0.35 or more	3,000 or more	13%

1995 data. In this case, however, two sets of national data were generated: cropland availability per person, and freshwater availability per person. For cropland, the following stress categories were used: where cropland availability was less than 0.07 hectares per person, countries were assumed to experience *extreme stress* conditions; from 0.07 to just less than 0.21 hectares per person, *high stress;* from 0.21 to just less than 0.35 hectares per person, *medium stress;* 0.35 hectares per person or more, *low stress.* For freshwater availability, the following categories were used: where freshwater availability was less than 1,000 cubic meters per person, countries were assumed to experience *extreme stress* conditions; from 1,000 to just less than 1,667 cubic meters per person, *high stress;* from 1,667 to just less than 3,000 cubic meters per person, *medium stress;* 3,000 cubic meters per person or more, *low stress.* [For additional information, see Appendix 2J.] After placing all countries in the most limiting category determined among both resources, the likelihood of civil conflict in each category was calculated as the percentage of countries that experienced civil conflict from 1990 to 2000.

Results of this analysis suggest a weak association between critical resource scarcity and the likelihood of civil conflict [Table 5.2]. Countries assumed to experience high or extreme demographic stress associated with cropland or renewable fresh water were about 1.5 times as likely to experience civil conflict in the 1990s than countries that did not fall into these categories (those still having more than 0.21 hectares of cropland per person, and more than 1,667 cubic meters of renewable fresh water per person).

The evidence from case studies suggests that shortages of cropland may be more closely associated with civil disturbances in low-income countries than shortages of fresh water, even though the latter resource is critical to all aspects of economic development. Perhaps because water is seen traditionally and legally as a community resource, local disputes over water rights most often evolve into complex legal disputes between local or provincial governments, and courts and water agencies have been surprisingly successful—so far—at defusing tensions around water scarcity. In contrast to water, land lends itself to longstanding private and inequitable ownership. And there are conflicting traditions of landholding. When cropland becomes locally scarce, peasants who recognize traditional ethnic communal rights to land tend to come into conflict with ethnically different landholders who have secured their holdings with title deeds or whose ancestors were granted land after conquest.

Calculations using 2005 population projections show that more than 30 countries have moved into the extreme stress category, falling below the most conservative benchmarks for either cropland

RECENT POPULATION GROWTH HAS BEEN RESPONSIBLE FOR THE STEADY INCREASE IN THE NUMBER OF COUNTRIES CLASSIFIED AS EXPERIENCING SCARCITY IN PER CAPITA AVAILABILITY OF CROPLAND, OR IN PER CAPITA AVAILABILITY OF RENEWABLE FRESH WATER.

(0.07 hectares per person) or renewable fresh water (1,000 cubic meters per person)—levels that analysts have called *scarcity*.[90] Most are in the arid Middle East and North Africa, where these natural resources are naturally limited by climate and where population growth has helped push demand to or beyond adequate supply [Maps 5.1, 5.2]. Other cropland-scarce countries (including Japan, Bangladesh and South Korea) and other water-scarce countries (including Burundi, Rwanda and Kenya) are humid temperate or tropical countries that have dropped below one of these per capita benchmarks largely as a result of population growth. While oil-producing and industrialized countries can afford to invest in technology and possess ample foreign currency to import grain, cropland-scarce and water-scarce countries with perennially weak economies and unstable governments are likely to endure intermittent local food shortages or to become chronic supplicants for food aid.

Even as UN demographers project declines in fertility for the foreseeable future—and they assume in making these scenarios that the needed government policies and family planning services will be in place in the coming decades—they also project continuing population growth during the next two decades in almost every developing country. In the coming decades, competition for cropland and fresh water are likely to grow increasingly intense in the most agrarian states, and challenge the capacities of governments to increase agricultural output and efficiently manage fresh water. Whatever the historical record, the outcomes of increasing competition for these critical resources and their implications for rural economic security are uncertain and less than reassuring.

■ **KEY POINT** Evidence from case studies suggests that the major sources of vulnerability to civil conflict that are associated with declines in available cropland and fresh water have been generated by the decreasing capacity of rural areas to maintain secure livelihoods and absorb growing labor forces. In the past, eruptions of civil tensions over cropland have been more common than over freshwater resources. While low per capita levels of land and water persist in several populous industrial countries, these countries—with their robust urban economies and well-run services—are much less vulnerable to civil conflict involving these resources.

■ **KEY POINT** Tensions between states over renewable natural resources have most often developed over rights to ocean fisheries and transboundary freshwater supplies. These tensions generally have led to interstate negotiations rather than warfare. Continued rapid population growth in the developing world, however, suggests a future unlike the past. The prospects for continued interstate cooperation, particularly over transboundary water rights, remain uncertain.

■ **KEY POINT** Countries in high or extreme demographic stress categories for cropland or renewable fresh water were about 1.5 times as likely to experience civil conflict in the 1990s as countries that did not fall into these categories, suggesting a weak association between worsening scarcities of these critical resources, by themselves, and an increased likelihood of civil conflict.

■ **POLICY PRESCRIPTION** Mediators of environmental disputes prescribe strategies for easing tensions over cropland and fresh water that include formalizing and enforcing unambiguous property rights, training resource managers and funding management and extension programs, pricing agricultural products fairly, and investing in programs that slow population growth.

BRIEFING POINTS Cropland and Fresh Water

CHAPTER SIX

Stress Factor Four: HIV/AIDS, Death in the Prime of Life

In contrast to the other factors, the case for the security relevance of the HIV/AIDS pandemic rests solely on the possible implications of the disease's growing demographic effects, rather than on historical data that suggest a relationship between the disease and increased risk of civil conflict. Even as recently as the early 1990s—the period that our analysis examines for these risks—the scale of AIDS mortality was significantly smaller than the 3 million people expected to die worldwide this year, or more to the point, far smaller than the toll projected for the near future.

The most worrisome of the hypothesized influences of AIDS is its deadly impact on a nation's trained workforce and its power to reshape a nation's age structure in an unprecedented way. The current severity of these effects worldwide is shown in the adjoining map, which uses as its indicator the proportion of death among all working-age adults, aged 15 to 64 years, over the years 2000 to 2005. AIDS-affected states also could become vulnerable to political instability in the future as the staggering number of children orphaned by the disease increases the proportion of dependent people, exacerbates poverty, widens inequalities, and erodes the operational readiness of military forces. The expected overall impact is a pernicious combination of deepening poverty in tandem with a loss of trust in governments that are increasingly unable to deliver basic services, let alone promote economic development.

Dying Young

No disease in human experience debilitates and kills exactly as AIDS does, laying low by the tens of millions not the weak and the old, but people in the most productive—and reproductive—decades

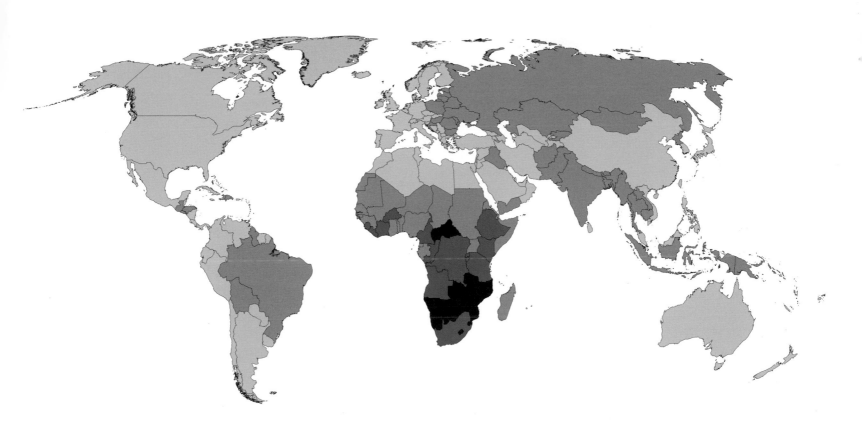

of their lives. The HIV connection to security stems largely from the fact that 90 percent of fatalities associated with the virus occur among people of working age. And where the epidemic is advanced, the disease is remarkably widespread, affecting the operations of government, the armed forces, schools, health care facilities, factories and farms.

The *most seriously AIDS-affected countries* (so categorized because more than 20 percent of their reproductive-age population is infected with the virus) today are Botswana, Zimbabwe, Swaziland, Lesotho, Namibia, Zambia and South Africa. These countries are now losing from 10 to 18 percent of their working-age population through premature death every five years. In comparison, industrial countries typically lose about 1 percent of those age groups to death every five years. Over the last half of the 1990s, war-torn countries with relatively low levels of HIV prevalence—such as Afghanistan, Sudan and Sri Lanka—experienced from 4 to 6 percent death in that age group.[91]

In heavily AIDS-affected countries, public agencies and private firms that provide health benefits and employ trained technicians and professionals are among the hardest hit. In South Africa, for example, employers experience what economists have called an AIDS "tax"—the sum of added expenditures for training new employees, for providing health care benefits and burial fees, and for frequent sick leave. Combined with the incalculable losses of managerial-level expertise, the AIDS tax can cripple agency budgets, whittle away profit margins and frighten off foreign investors.[92]

Technicians and professionals who travel on the job appear doubly at risk of contracting HIV. Studies show that sexually transmitted HIV can spread first through employed and educated groups, though its prevalence often plateaus at lower levels than in poorer communities.[93] Those whose jobs

MAP 6.1

WORKING-AGE DEATHS, 2000–05

Death as a Proportion of the Working-Age Population, Over a Five Year Period

DEMOGRAPHIC STRESS CATEGORY

- EXTREME: 10% OR GREATER
- HIGH: 7% TO LESS THAN 10%
- MEDIUM: 2% TO LESS THAN 7%
- LOW: LESS THAN 2%
- NO DATA

DATA SOURCE: UNITED NATIONS POPULATION DIVISION, 2003

FIGURE 6.1

BOTSWANA'S AGE STRUCTURE IN 2020

With and Without the AIDS Epidemic

High HIV prevalence in Botswana (and in other sub-Saharan African countries) threatens to produce an unprecedented age structure with a large youth bulge and an unusually small proportion of older adults. The shape of the AIDS-induced age structure (red, interior bottle-like profile) reflects high premature death rates among adults, rising childhood mortality, and declines in births that are influenced by illness and death among reproductive-age women. The black exterior profile shows the projected age structure had there been no AIDS epidemic in the country.

■ WITH AIDS

■ WITHOUT AIDS

DATA SOURCE: US CENSUS BUREAU, 1999

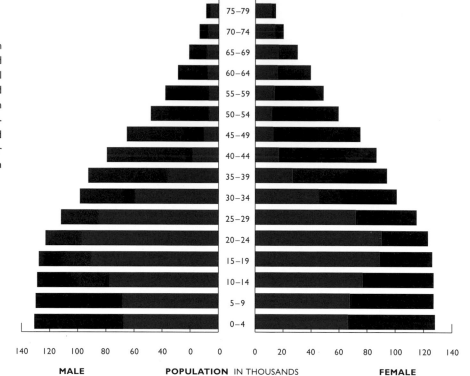

require extended periods of travel away from home—in developing countries these tend to be mostly men who work as miners, professionals such as agricultural extension technicians or water engineers, truck drivers, soldiers and seamen—are among the groups most at risk. Wives, lovers and newborns of these become part of a wider circle of infection.[94] Loss of technicians and professionals is weakening major economic and social sectors—including health care and education, policing and water distribution—in the heavily AIDS-affected countries. Lacking sufficient capacity to plan for and resolve long-term problems and to respond to acute crises, these states risk stalling in their paths toward industrialization, democracy and the final phases of the demographic transition.

The Demographic Impacts of HIV/AIDS

The outsized impact of HIV/AIDS on mortality has emerged as a demographic force in southern Africa. Recent projections by UN demographers show births more than offsetting AIDS deaths in most of the 53 countries that UN demographers now consider *AIDS-affected* (49 countries with HIV prevalence at 1 percent or greater, plus Russia, United States, India and China). In the seven most seriously AIDS-affected countries named above, however, deaths are projected to overtake births and cause population decreases in the next few years.[95]

Tragically, some of the most dramatic slowing in population growth rates is occurring in countries such as South Africa and Botswana that have experienced both high rates of HIV prevalence and significant declines in fertility. Unlike the birthrate-driven slowing of population growth that proved economically beneficial to East and Southeast Asian states late in the 20th century—known as the

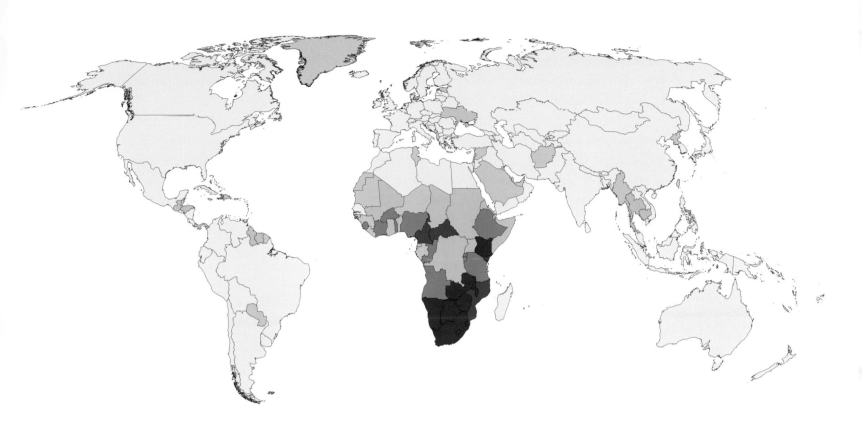

demographic bonus (see Chapter 2)—slowed population growth in southern Africa due to deaths from AIDS is leading to an ominous, bottle-shaped population age structure likely to hinder rather than help economic growth [Figure 6.1].[96]

AIDS Orphans and Poverty

The combination of high levels of HIV infection, high fertility and the lack of access to proven antiretroviral therapies has left AIDS-affected countries with millions of orphaned children (defined by the United Nations as those aged less than 15 years who have lost one or both natural parents).[97] Eleven million of the world's 14 million AIDS orphans live in Africa.[98] Extended family networks of close and distant relatives, many of them elderly, are taking over much of the burden of child care in African countries when AIDS breaks up families. Such caregivers are not always physically or economically capable of providing sufficient care for children.[99] Many orphans suffer neglect or abuse in their new homes. Many drop out of school early.[100] And some end up living on city streets.

Urban street children were a concern for the public health and criminal justice systems in many developing countries even before HIV/AIDS reached epidemic proportions. AIDS orphans are substantially augmenting the population of children on city streets. In Nairobi, Kenya, where at least 30,000 homeless children roam the city, this destitute population is expected to grow at an estimated 10 percent annually. Out of school and living in ruthlessly hierarchical groups, Nairobi's street children spend their days begging, scavenging, sniffing glue and engaging in petty theft.[101] Lacking in formal education and skills that could be used to secure formal-sector employment, street children

MAP 6.2

ADULT HIV PREVALENCE, 2001

Proportion of Reproductive-age Population (Aged 15 to 49 Years) Living with HIV

■ 15% OR MORE

■ 10% TO LESS THAN 15%

■ 5% TO LESS THAN 10%

▨ 1% TO LESS THAN 5%

□ LESS THAN 1%

▨ NO DATA

DATA SOURCE: UNITED NATIONS JOINT PROGRAMME ON HIV/AIDS, 2002

often find themselves recruited into organized crime or used as child soldiers. Without efforts to place these children in families and keep them in school, they may grow into a source of abused and unemployed malcontents ready to join insurgencies against the state, or to be used by oppressive states to carry out their own violent agendas.

While HIV/AIDS has permeated all economic classes in AIDS-affected countries, studies suggest that the disease disproportionately disrupts the lives and communities of the poor. Protracted illness and death of the breadwinner typically deplete savings, and often lead to a change of residence, the withdrawal of children from school, and a deterioration of health conditions among youngsters who survive.[102] In countries where women lack rights of inheritance, young women widowed by AIDS often lose their land, livestock and children, and then migrate to cities to take menial jobs or become sex workers. Illness and deaths from AIDS in households engaged in small-scale farming appear to have exacerbated malnutrition during recent drought conditions in southern Africa. Hopelessness among low-income groups could produce situations where insurgent organizations might be seen as the most viable means of obtaining economic relief and social mobility.

HIV/AIDS in the Military

Recent reporting of HIV-surveillance among military units has alerted national leaders to the peril the epidemic poses to the strength and integrity of armed forces. Where security forces are now experiencing exceedingly high HIV prevalence, several analysts envision growing possibilities for civil breakdowns.[103] The limited available data suggest that in the armed forces of as many as 20 developing countries, more than 15 percent of total force strength is HIV-positive.[104] Nearly all of these countries are in sub-Saharan Africa, where in some cases more than half of military personnel could

---

TABLE 6.1

HIV PREVALENCE IN SELECTED MILITARIES IN SUB-SAHARAN AFRICA

The military forces of AIDS-affected countries are experiencing debilitating rates of HIV prevalence. The rate of infection for sexually transmitted diseases in military forces worldwide is generally at least twice that of civilians, and HIV is no exception. AIDS-related illness and death have prompted commands in several countries to downgrade the readiness of their units, and forced changes in operations and deployment plans.

DATA SOURCE: DEFENSE INTELLIGENCE AGENCY, 2000

Country	Estimated HIV Prevalence percent
Congo, Democratic Republic	40–60%
Tanzania	15–30
Liberia	10–20
Congo, Republic	10–25
Côte d'Ivoire	10–20
Ghana	4–15

be HIV-positive [Table 6.1].[105] Intelligence analysts report that AIDS-related illness and death in enlisted ranks and officer corps has forced military leaders in Malawi, Nigeria, Rwanda, South Africa, Zambia and Zimbabwe to modify operational schedules, or to downgrade their assessment of the operational strength or readiness of units under their command.[106]

When military training and health units fail to address HIV among troops, armed forces can turn into mobile reservoirs of infection that influence the course of the epidemic in their home communities, throughout their own countries and in those countries to which they are deployed. Without HIV-prevention education and affordable condoms, demobilization and reintegration of combatants almost anywhere in sub-Saharan Africa is a potential public health crisis.[107]

While health policymakers have expressed concerns about the possible role that lengthy peacekeeping deployments may play in accelerating the spread of the disease, there are few avenues for change. For example, hefty payments to states for contributing peacekeepers, critics claim, create a disincentive for contributor states to collect data on HIV prevalence—the results of which could undermine these troops' participation.[108] A United Nations Security Council resolution encourages states to adopt long-term strategies within their armed forces for HIV/AIDS education, condom distribution and other means of prevention, voluntary and confidential testing and counseling, and treatment of their personnel, as part of their preparation for participation in peacekeeping operations.[109]

Risk Assessment: Prospects for the Pandemic

While there should be little doubt as to the seriousness of demographic and social influences threatening to arise from the HIV/AIDS pandemic, is there evidence yet that this disease puts states at risk of civil conflict? To address this question for the 1990s, countries were assigned to four demographic stress categories, based upon the proportion of deaths that occurred among working-age adults over a five-year period, from 1995 to 2000. [For additional details, see Appendix 2K.] The following stress categories were used: where the five-year death toll among working-age adults was greater than precisely 10.0 percent of this group, countries were assumed to experience *extreme stress* conditions; from 7.0 percent to just less than 10.0 percent, *high stress;* from 2.0 percent to less than 7.0 percent, *medium stress;* less than 2.0 percent, *low stress.*

Our analysis found countries in the extreme and high categories were too few to claim a discernible association between the countrywide rate of adult death, by itself, and the incidence of civil conflict during the 1990s. Deaths resulting from the HIV/AIDS pandemic, however, have yet to reach their peak. The first decade of the 21st century may offer a test of the hypothesis we venture here: that those countries with the highest rates of adult deaths due to AIDS [Map 6.1] will be statistically more likely than countries with low rates to experience new civil conflicts.

Uncertainties cloud the future of AIDS. No acceptable vaccine is imminent, and promising vaginal microbicides still face years of testing. If proven effective and safe, such microbicides would offer a female-controlled preventive method that would kill the virus before it could infect.[110] For the foreseeable future, however, condoms for men and for women [see endnote, describing the *female condom*][111] are the only technologies available for protection from sexually transmitted HIV and from other sexually transmitted infections, which are known to increase the risk of HIV transmission three- to four-fold.[112] The current supply of donated male condoms in sub-Saharan Africa, however,

WITHOUT HIV-PREVENTION EDUCATION AND AFFORDABLE CONDOMS, DEMOBILIZATION AND REINTEGRATION OF COMBATANTS ALMOST ANYWHERE IN SUB-SAHARAN AFRICA IS A POTENTIAL PUBLIC HEALTH CRISIS.

has been estimated at fewer than five per man per year.[113] Governments continue to negotiate, often from a weak position, with pharmaceutical companies over the prices and quality of drugs used in AIDS treatments. And scientists have identified several strains of HIV that are resistant to some of the drugs that once successfully suppressed the virus.

Experts can now only guess how the disease will evolve and when its prevalence will peak and start to decline. To generate the United Nation's 2002 population projections, UN demographers assumed that the disease's current growth rates will continue until 2010, after which the incidence of HIV will begin to decline gradually in every country, presumably due to accumulating preventive efforts.[114]

Several countries have made progress in combating the pandemic. Senegal, Brazil and Thailand all have significantly reduced rates of HIV infection, and in Uganda HIV prevalence has fallen by more than half. These countries have pushed the disease back largely by facing the facts of the pandemic squarely, educating the public about its spread, and promoting a combination of sexual restraint and the use of condoms in non-monogamous sexual relations (thus, the acronym: *ABC*, for "Abstain until marriage, or Be faithful to a single sexual partner, or use a Condom"). Far more governments, however, remain inert or ineffectual, in some cases even denying the disease is an issue for them. The virus appears to be spreading rapidly through high-risk groups in Russia, Nigeria, China and India, without any indication that these populous and strategically important states are mounting an adequate response. A recent report by the National Intelligence Council made pessimistic conclusions about the course of the pandemic in these countries, which the report's authors dubbed the "next wave" of HIV infection.[115]

Despite the explicit role of military forces in state and regional stability, programs that reduce military personnel's risks of contracting and spreading HIV have moved slowly and remain relatively poorly funded in most AIDS-affected countries. Because of inflexible assistance restrictions and agency biases, donor countries have missed opportunities to promote HIV/AIDS education and prevention through international military-to-military, civilian-to-military and military-to-civilian programs of cooperation.[116] And while armed forces have generally outpaced private companies and civilian government agencies in facilitating HIV/AIDS awareness, still only eight out of ten militaries surveyed worldwide report that they promote condom use, and far fewer actually distribute them.[117]

During the 1990s, the political will and financial resources mobilized for effective HIV/AIDS prevention and education in the poorest countries were inadequate. According to some projections, well-run prevention efforts could do more to reduce AIDS mortality than either vaccines or drug treatments—if they begin in earnest in the current decade.[118] The United Nations Population Fund estimated that, by the year 2000, international donors should have been providing at least 8 billion condoms annually to reduce significantly the rate of HIV infection in the developing world and Eastern Europe. Instead they offered fewer than 1 billion.[119] Despite a recent large-scale U.S. initiative that could greatly expand funding for both HIV prevention and AIDS treatment,[120] the world has only raised about half of the $10.5 billion that experts estimate is needed annually by 2005 to deal adequately with HIV prevention, AIDS treatment and care in low- and middle-income countries.[121]

■ **KEY POINT** In sub-Saharan Africa, where the HIV/AIDS pandemic has hit hardest, countries are experiencing debilitating rates of illness and death among technicians and professionals in the private sector, in public services and in the military. These losses threaten to erode the functional capacity of some of the world's weakest states and could significantly hamper their abilities to develop economically, and to respond to chronic domestic discontent and sudden crises.

■ **KEY POINT** Over the next two decades a wave of AIDS-related deaths among working-age adults in the seven worst AIDS-affected countries is likely to produce population age structures never before seen in history, with the numbers of old and very young predominating over those of the working-age population. These age structures seem likely to foster the potential for political instability.

■ **KEY POINT** AIDS orphans—now 14 million globally, 11 million of them in sub-Saharan Africa alone—are swelling the ranks of street children in the cities of developing countries. These children are more than a human tragedy. They are a likely source of future urban discontent, criminal activity, and recruits for insurgencies or police states. Government support for placing homeless orphans in families and in schools could help reduce future risks.

■ **POLICY PRESCRIPTION** Military forces in about 20 African and Asian countries appear to have extraordinarily high HIV prevalence rates, posing threats to their operational readiness, to peacekeeping commitments, and to communities with which they come in contact. A few HIV/AIDS education and prevention programs in the armed forces of developing countries—Uganda, Senegal, Morocco, Tanzania and Thailand—have produced notable results. Such efforts should be multiplied by increasing funding to international military-to-military, civilian-to-military and military-to-civilian HIV/AIDS programs.

■ **POLICY PRESCRIPTION** Only significantly expanded prevention efforts, or a massive mobilization of treatment programs, or an unforeseen vaccine breakthrough, or some combination of all three of these is likely to stave off major demographic changes and disruptive losses of human capital in countries seriously affected by AIDS. Public health specialists recommend a massive international effort giving equal weight to HIV prevention and AIDS treatment programs in each of these states. It is essential that these involve promotion and supply of condoms to all who could benefit from their use, including military personnel.

CHAPTER SEVEN

Interactions of Demographic Stress Factors

Several researchers have found one or more of the demographic stress factors examined in this report—high proportions of young adults, rapid urban population growth, diminishing per capita supplies of cropland and fresh water, and high rates of death among working-age adults (largely a result of the HIV/AIDS pandemic)—to compound or otherwise interact with each other. Many countries' populations are characterized by more than one factor. These interacting effects are the focus of this chapter's three-part analysis, and they are the basis for the report's global projections of the demographic risks of civil conflict, 2000 to 2010. These projections are featured on the adjoining color-coded global map [Map 7] and table [Table 7.1], entitled Demographic Risks of Civil Conflict, 2000 to 2010.

The first part of this analysis, discussed in the following section, consists of a brief review of interactions relevant to conflict among the demographic risk factors explored in this report, and it provides background and justification for the parts of the analysis that follow. The second part of the analysis tests the central thesis of this report. This part sets out to determine if countries experiencing multiple demographic risks were actually more vulnerable to post-Cold War civil conflict than those measured with fewer or no apparent demographic risks—and it finds that they were. The results of the latter calculations provide a foundation for the third and final part of this report's centerpiece analysis. Using the current status of the demographic factors studied in this report, this analysis generates a list of countries that appear at high levels of population-related risk of civil conflict during the current decade—from 2000 to 2010.

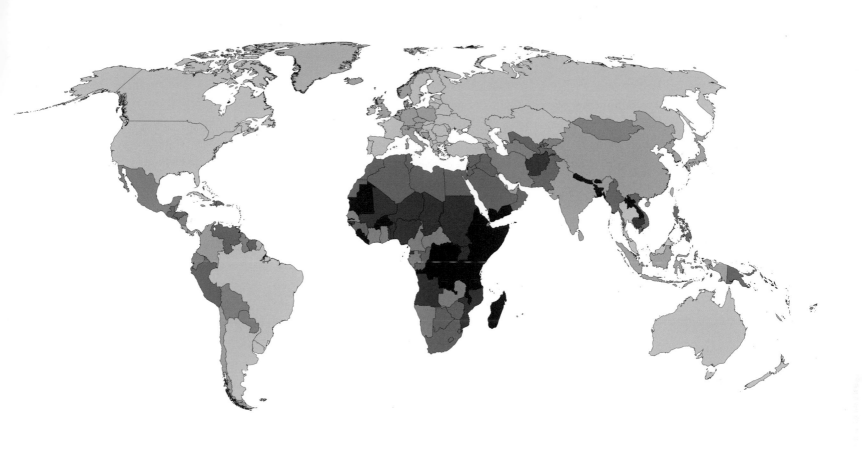

MAP 7

DEMOGRAPHIC STRESS, 2000–10

During the current decade, the most dangerous overlaps of civil-conflict-related demographic stress factors are concentrated primarily in sub-Saharan Africa and in the Middle East. A few zones of risk are scattered across southern Asia and, to a lesser extent, in parts of Latin America. In this map, countries are highlighted according to the type (or combination of types) of factors that are in high or extreme categories of demographic stress as of 2005. As a guide to the risks associated with these combinations of stress factors, see Table 7.1, which provides estimates of the likelihood of civil conflict for these combinations during the previous period (1990–2000).

RISK ASSESSMENT	DEMOGRAPHIC STRESS FACTORS
VERY HIGH RISK	**3 FACTORS:** LARGE YOUTH BULGE, RAPID URBAN GROWTH, AND LOW CROPLAND OR FRESHWATER AVAILABILITY
HIGH RISK	**2 FACTORS:** LARGE YOUTH BULGE AND RAPID URBAN GROWTH
HIGH RISK	**2 FACTORS:** LARGE YOUTH BULGE, AND LOW CROPLAND OR FRESHWATER AVAILABILITY
ELEVATED RISK	**1 FACTOR:** LARGE YOUTH BULGE
	1 FACTOR: LOW CROPLAND OR FRESHWATER AVAILABILITY
	NO APPARENT DEMOGRAPHIC STRESS (AMONG FACTORS STUDIED)
	NO DATA

Interactions

Presumably, multiple demographic risk factors pose challenges to governments that exceed in scale and complexity the challenges of single factors. Interacting and operating in tandem, multiple risk factors spread tensions and grievances more widely, both geographically and among ethnic and socio-economic groups, than any single factor. Thus, the occurrence of multiple demographic risks could explain why countries in the early stages of demographic transition are so prone to civil conflicts, and why progress along the transition reduces that vulnerability.

Several studies demonstrate that rapid urban population growth, for example, tends to be marked by a localized preponderance of young adults who leave behind more traditional lifestyles in rural areas and migrate to cities seeking work, education and urban amenities. In East and South Asia and in Latin America, the increasing subdivision of farmland among larger populations—often exacerbated by declining soil productivity, controlled food prices, and lack of access to credit—appears to have provided some of the impetus for a youthful migration to the cities. Similarly, in most of the Middle East, North Africa and the arid reaches of India and Pakistan, declines in per capita fresh water are adding a stimulus for young adults to resettle in urban areas.[122] Unusually large urban youth bulges probably facilitated massive student and worker rioting in several Asian countries during the 1960s and 1970s, and are likely contributing to the communal conflicts that have erupted more recently in the cities of northern India and Pakistan.[123]

Demographic factors also interact to amplify the effects of the HIV/AIDS epidemic. Rural-to-urban migrants and AIDS orphans are among the groups with a high risk of contracting HIV. And because of the eight-year-or-longer interval between HIV infection and AIDS-related death, high rates of infection among young adults tend to distort age structures in ways that actually increase the size of the youth bulge. [See Figure 6.1, preceding chapter.][124] This effect threatens to further increase the youth bulge in sub-Saharan Africa, where UN demographers estimate that about half of all adults are presently between the ages of 15 and 29 years.

Multiple Risks and Post-Cold War Conflicts

A second phase of this analysis sheds light on whether countries experiencing multiple demographic risks were actually more vulnerable to post-Cold War civil conflict than those measured with fewer or no apparent demographic risks [Table 7.1]. This phase consists of overlapping the countries in the high or extreme demographic stress categories—what are called, in this analysis, the *critical categories* [for additional information, see Appendix 2L]—for the demographic factors found to be associated with outbreaks of civil conflict during the 1990s: the proportion of young adults in 1995, the rate of urban population growth from 1990 to 1995, and the per capita availability of either cropland or fresh water in 1995. By the mid-1990s, the HIV/AIDS pandemic had not yet progressed to the alarming rates of prevalence and premature death now experienced in southern African countries, and the countries in critical categories were still too few to evaluate the influence of the fourth factor: death rates among working-age adults. Thus, this factor is omitted from the analysis (although this factor is indicated on Table 7.2.

For each country, the number of demographic stress factors that had values in critical categories was identified (either zero, one, two or three factors) for the 1990s. The likelihood of outbreaks of civil conflict was calculated for groups of countries with each of the possible overlaps (for groups with a minimum of 20 countries), and a profile produced for those multiple factors [Table 7.1]. During this period, 66 countries out of a total of 145 without continuing or reemerging conflicts fell into more than one critical category. And these multiple-stress countries accounted for 23 out of the 36 countries with new outbreaks of civil conflicts—about two-thirds of the total—during the 1990s.

A Decade of Risk: 2000 to 2010

The hypothesis that underlies this analysis is that the influence of the demographic risk factors is real and significant and that this association between overlapping factors and the likelihood of conflict will continue into the future. In this section, the same method is used to identify countries that are projected, by 2005, to have crossed into the critical categories of risk for each of the three demographic factors analyzed. The overlaps of critical levels are identified on the adjoining map, and the 25 countries with three overlaps are listed along with their values for demographic stress factors [Table 7.2].

Out of 180 countries analyzed—with and without prior conflict, and with populations over 150,000—this analysis identified 76 states in two or three critical categories of the three demographic

---

TABLE 7.1

DEMOGRAPHIC STRESS FACTORS AND THE LIKELIHOOD OF CIVIL CONFLICT, 1990–2000

Countries with a large youth bulge, as a group, had a higher likelihood of civil conflict than other countries during the 1990s, and this likelihood increased in the presence of rapid urban population growth and low availability of cropland or fresh water. This relationship helps explain the association between progress along the demographic transition and declines in the likelihood of conflict during that decade. In this analysis, countries with a large youth bulge and one other demographic stress were combined into a single category (the high risk category) to compensate for an inadequate sample size of countries with both a large youth bulge and rapid urban growth. While countries with both a large youth bulge and low per capita availability of cropland or fresh water experienced more than twice the likelihood of civil conflict, low availability of these natural resources by itself was not associated with this type of conflict. A fourth factor—working-age adult deaths, largely reflecting the influence of the HIV/AIDS pandemic—is not included in this analysis. The data used excludes conflicts that persisted or reemerged from the late 1980s.

Risk Category	Number of Countries	Demographic Stress Factors			Likelihood of an Outbreak of Civil Conflict 1990–2000
		FACTOR 1	FACTOR 2	FACTOR 3	
Very High Risk	25	Large Youth Bulge	Rapid Urban Population Growth	Low Cropland or Freshwater Availability	40%
High Risk	40	Large Youth Bulge	Rapid Urban Population Growth OR	Low Cropland or Freshwater Availability	33%
Elevated Risk	21	Large Youth Bulge (only)	—	—	24%
	26	—	—	Low Cropland or Freshwater Availability (only)	12%
	31	—	—	—	16%

TABLE 7.2

FOR 2000 TO 2010, 25 COUNTRIES ARE ASSESSED WITH VERY HIGH LEVELS OF DEMOGRAPHIC RISK OF CIVIL CONFLICT

Each of these 25 high-risk countries (ordered alphabetically) are in the high or extreme categories of stress in three or more of the demographic factors on which the analysis focused. These factors were previously determined (in Chapters 3 to 6) to be associated with an elevated likelihood of civil conflict during the 1990s. Working-age deaths (high levels occur in the AIDS-affected countries) were not used to determine this list. However, 10 countries among these 25 are in the high or extreme stress category of this demographic factor, probably contributing additional risk.

	Young Adults (aged 15–29 years)	Urban Population Growth	Cropland Availability	Fresh Water Availability	Working-Age Adult Death
Year	2005	2000–05	2005	2005	2000–05
Units of Measure	Percent of All Adults (aged 15 years and older)	Percent per Year	Hectares per Person	Cubic Meters per Person	Percent Over 5-year Period
Bangladesh	45.6%	4.3%	0.06	7,936	2.9%
Bhutan	47.7	5.9	0.07	39,719	2.8
Burkina Faso	55.1	5.1	0.28	942	7.0
Burundi	55.6	6.4	0.17	547	8.9
Comoros	50.2	4.6	0.16	nd	2.9
Congo, Democratic Republic	52.3	4.9	0.14	22,878	7.4
East Timor	49.0	4.7	0.09	nd	5.8
Eritrea	51.0	6.3	0.11	1,346	5.7
Ethiopia	50.3	4.6	0.14	1,483	7.1
Gambia	44.4	4.4	0.16	5,336	4.6
Kenya	55.5	4.6	0.14	913	9.3
Laos	47.4	4.6	0.16	56,435	3.8
Liberia	52.0	6.8	0.17	64,394	7.9
Madagascar	48.0	4.9	0.19	18,307	4.0
Malawi	51.2	4.6	0.18	1,352	11.2
Maldives	49.9	4.6	0.01	nd	1.9
Mauritania	47.4	5.1	0.16	3,585	4.2
Nepal	45.5	5.1	0.11	7,988	3.2
Occupied Palestinian Territory	48.8	4.1	0.06	nd	1.2
Rwanda	53.5	4.2	0.13	581	9.6
Sierra Leone	48.3	6.3	0.10	29,965	9.5
Solomon Islands	49.0	6.0	0.12	89,214	1.6
Somalia	50.8	5.8	0.10	1,303	4.8
Tanzania	53.1	5.3	0.13	2,372	8.6
Yemen	53.2	5.3	0.08	186	3.0

nd = NO DATA AVAILABLE.

VALUES IN **RED** INDICATE HIGH OR EXTREME DEMOGRAPHIC STRESS.

stress factors identified in our analysis (a high proportion of youth, rapid urban population growth, or diminished per capita availability of fresh water or cropland). Of this set of countries, 51 are characterized by just two demographic stress factors, while 25 have reached critical categories in all three of these factors. Most of the 25 very-high-risk states are in sub-Saharan Africa, the major world region in the earliest stages of the demographic transition, including the Democratic Republic of the Congo, Liberia, Sierra Leone, Rwanda, Ethiopia and Eritrea. Compounding the concerns about this region is the fact that 10 of these nations also face high adult death rates during this decade related mostly to the HIV/AIDS pandemic. Several countries in Asia also have reached critical levels in all three major demographic stress factors, including Yemen, Nepal, East Timor, Laos, Bangladesh and (though not an independent state) the Occupied Palestinian Territories. Latin America and the Caribbean include no countries with three stress factors, but El Salvador, Haiti, Venezuela, Guatemala, and Peru are among the countries with two. Iraq, Afghanistan, Pakistan and Saudi Arabia—four countries of considerable interest related to the recruitment into, or activity of, organizations associated with the al Qaeda network—all are in two critical categories of demographic risk of conflict.

Several features of this list are especially noteworthy. Each state that appears on the list of critical levels of two or more demographic stress factors has first reached a critical level in its proportion of youth—where young adults, aged 15 to 29 years, comprise more than 40 percent of all adults. Fully three-quarters of the states in sub-Saharan Africa experience two or three demographic stress factors, as do one-fourth of those in the Middle East and North African regions. About one-fifth of all South and Central Asian states and almost as large a proportion of states in Latin America and the Caribbean region can be characterized in this same way (though limited to countries with two stress factors in the Western Hemisphere).

A weakness of this demographic analysis lies in its treatment of geographically large states. Because it is based solely on national data, the analysis does not reflect high intensities of these demographic factors at the sub-national level—where data are difficult to obtain. Sub-national and ethnic population factors are probably an important consideration in most large countries, including Brazil, China, India, Indonesia and Russia.

Despite the current lack of certainty about the ultimate influence of HIV/AIDS on the vulnerability of states to conflict, the potential risk of its demographic effects, too, deserve consideration. Twenty-three countries, all of them in sub-Saharan Africa, have reached critical levels of working-age adult death. This emerging and still speculative factor is largely a product of the AIDS pandemic, with levels augmented by warfare, other infectious diseases, and various other disasters. Working-age adult death is projected—over the 2000 to 2005 period—to attain critical levels, exceeding 7 percent losses every five years, in 10 of the 25 countries already burdened by the other three risk factors. In several countries, that five-year death toll is projected to exceed 13 percent.

Some states will deal with these demographic challenges in the coming decade, and avoid civil conflict. Most of the countries that this study shows at high demographic risk, however, lack the capacity to adequately respond to these challenges. During the research phase of this report, anti-government violence erupted in several high-risk countries—the Solomon Islands (with critical levels in three risk factors), Madagascar (in three factors), and Côte d'Ivoire (in one factor, but an extremely high proportion of young adults and high rates of working-age adult mortality). Alarmingly, some of today's greatest demographic challenges are among states already caught in vicious cycles of civil conflict and state failure. For example, decades of civil war in Afghanistan (with critical levels in two risk factors), Liberia (in three factors) and Cambodia (in three factors) have destroyed much of the infrastructure, human capital and organizational capacity that in past decades might have been potent resources for conflict prevention and resolution. It is difficult to imagine any of these demographically-at-risk states making lasting strides in democratization or economic liberalization without alleviating some of their vulnerability through progress along the demographic transition.

Working Toward the Security Demographic

This report and its analyses have investigated a set of high-risk demographic characteristics that, significant evidence suggests, puts stress on the political systems of more than one-third of the world's states, most of them in Africa, the Middle East and parts of South and Central Asia and Central America. In large part, these characteristics are an outgrowth of conditions typical of populations in the early and middle phases of the demographic transition—the transformation of societies from those where people live relatively short lives and have large families, to those where people live long lives and are raised in small, better educated and healthier families.

Near the endpoint of this transition are countries with demographic characteristics that our analysis identifies as a *security demographic*. These are characteristics that produce slowly or non-growing populations with mature—and likely less politically volatile—age structures, favoring more adequate support for children and greater household savings. Such characteristics make it easier for developing countries to improve the quality of health and education services, to build and maintain the infrastructure needed for social progress and economic growth, and to enable high employment rates that help give meaning to life as well as provide essential livelihood and strengthen government legitimacy.

Over the past 40 years, the scale of this demographic progress has been impressive but globally uneven. Indeed, most of the developing world is moving toward the security demographic—but there are alarming exceptions to this trend, and formidable challenges that lie in the path of full completion. Governments must work harder to reach all people, especially the young, with reproductive health services and information. They must work harder to educate and improve the status of women. And the world must overcome the HIV/AIDS pandemic. To continue declines in birthrates and increases in life expectancy in some of the poorest, most poorly governed, and most conflict-torn countries will require much more active international collaboration and far more political will than are evident today. Yet, as the close-knit relationship between demographic trends and civil conflict demonstrate in the post-Cold War years, few objectives could do more to bring about a global future of peace, security and economic development.

■ **KEY POINT** Key demographic characteristics that increase the risk of civil conflict interact with each other and with non-demographic factors, compounding net risk for countries in the early or middle phases of demographic transition. Multiple demographic stress factors tend to exacerbate each others' effects, expose more of a population and more geographic areas to tensions, and test developing-country governments with complex challenges.

■ **KEY POINT** Based on UN population data, 25 countries have reached critical levels (high or extreme stress) in three of the demographic factors considered in this report. Most are in sub-Saharan Africa, with most of the rest in Asia. Fifty-one countries in two critical-level categories also include countries in Latin America, the Caribbean and Pacific Islands.

■ **KEY POINT** Ten countries that have reached critical levels in three demographic factors also are experiencing excessive adult mortality, mostly due to high HIV prevalence. Perhaps because prevalence was lower in the 1990s and AIDS mortality lags nearly a decade behind an upsurge in HIV infection, statistical evidence for including working-age mortality as a risk was weak. Nonetheless, our review of this factor suggests that AIDS-associated risks are likely.

■ **POLICY PRESCRIPTION** Despite momentous progress along the demographic transition in the last 30 years by many developing countries—mostly in East Asia, the Caribbean and Latin America—more than one-third of the world's countries remain in the early and middle phases of the demographic transition. Those that lag appear likely to sustain high risks of civil conflict for years to come. As such, few have hopes for sustaining democratization or economic liberalization. Governments can promote progress through the demographic transition by improving the quality of and access to reproductive health information and services, by improving the status of women, and by working to overcome the HIV/AIDS pandemic.

ENDNOTES

[1] Moller H. Youth as a Force in the Modern World. *Comparative Studies in Society and History* 10: 237–260 (1967/68); Choucri N. *Population Dynamics and International Violence: Propositions, Insights and Evidence.* Cambridge, MA: MIT Press, 1973; Choucri N. *Population Dynamics and International Violence.* Lexington, MA: Lexington Press, 1974; Choucri N (ed). *Multidisciplinary Perspectives on Population and Conflict.* Syracuse: Syracuse Univ. Press, 1984.

[2] National Security Council. "Implications of Worldwide Population Growth for U.S. Security and Overseas Interests," National Security Study Memorandum 200. Washington, DC: NSC, 1974 (declassified July 3, 1989); Green M, Fearey R. World Population: The Silent Explosion. *Department of State Bulletin* (Fall): 1–32, 1978; Population Crisis Committee (PCC). World Population Growth and Global Security. *Population* 13 (Sept): 1–8 (1983); Barnett PG. "Population Pressures—Threat to Democracy," Wall chart. PCC: Washington, DC, 1989.

[3] Nichiporuk B. "The Security Dynamics of Demographic Factors," MR-1088-WFHF/RF/ DLPF/A. 52. Santa Monica: RAND, 2000; Homer-Dixon T, Percival V. "Environmental Scarcity and Violent Conflict: Briefing Book," Project on Environment, Population and Security (Smith B, series ed). Washington, DC: American Association for the Advancement of Science, 1996; International Crisis Group (IGC). "HIV/AIDS as a Security Issue," IGC Issue Report; Matthew RA. Environmental Stress and Human Security in Northern Pakistan. *Environmental Change and Security Project Report* 7: 17–31 (2001).

[4] Ministry of Defence (MOD). *The Future Strategic Context for Defence.* London: United Kingdom MOD, 2000; Directorate of Intelligence. "The United States and the Third World Century: How Much Will Demographics Stress Geopolitics?" OTI IA 2002-014. Washington, DC: Central Intelligence Agency, 2002; Directorate of Intelligence. "Long-term Global Demographic Trends: Reshaping the Geopolitical Landscape," OTI IA 2001–045. Washington, DC: Central Intelligence Agency, 2001; National Intelligence Council (NIC). "Global Trends 2015: A Dialogue About the Future With Non-government Experts," NIC 2000–02. Washington, DC: National Foreign Intelligence Board (NFIB), 2000; NIC. "The Global Infectious Disease Threat and Its Implications for the United States," NIE 99–17D. Washington, DC: NFIB, 2000; NIC. "Growing Global Migration and Its Implications for the United States," NIE 2001–02D. Washington, DC: NFIB, 2001.

[5] These data appear on the project's Website (a portion is listed in this report's appendix) and in several articles published in the *Journal of Peace Research.* Gleditsch NP, Wallensteen P, Eriksson M, Sollenberg M, Strand H. Armed Conflict 1946–2001: A New Dataset. *Journal of Peace Research* 39(5): 615–637 (2002); Wallensteen P, Sollenberg M. Armed Conflict, 1989–2000. *Journal of Peace* Research 38(5): 629–644 (2001); Wallensteen P, Sollenberg M. Armed Conflict and Conflict Complexes, 1989–97. *Journal of Peace Research* 35(5): 621– 634 (1998).

[6] UN Population Division. *World Population Prospects: The 2002 Revision,* POP/DB/WPP/Rev.2002/3/ F1. New York: United Nations, Dept. of Economic and Social Affairs, 2003; UN Population Division. *World Urbanization Prospects: The 2001 Revision,* POP/DB/WUP/Rev.2001. New York: United Nations, Dept. of Economic and Social Affairs, 2002.

[7] Zakaria F. *The Future of Freedom.* New York: W.W. Norton, 2003; Mansfield ED, Snyder J. Democratization and the Danger of War. *International Security* 20(1): 5–38 (1995), (note: data from Polity II data set and Correlates of War data); Esty DC and others. State Failure Task Force Report: Phase II Findings. *Environmental Change & Security Report* 5: 49–72 (1999), (note: data from Polity II data set); Gurr, TR, Marshall MG, Khosla D. *Peace and Conflict 2001: A Global Survey of Armed Conflicts, Self-Determination Movements, and Democracy.* College Park: Center for International Development and Conflict Management, Univ. of Maryland, 2001.

[8] Collier P. *Breaking the Conflict Trap: Civil War and Development Policy.* Washington, DC: World Bank and Oxford University Press, 2003.

9 Esty DC and others. State Failure Task Force Report: Phase II Findings. *Environmental Change & Security Report*, 5: 49–72 (1999); Ferguson N. *The Pity of War: Explaining World War I*. New York: Basic Books (1999); Barnett TPM. The Pentagon's New Map. *Esquire* (March), 174–179 (2003).

10 Gurr TR, Marshall MG, Khosla D. "Peace and Conflict 2001: A Global Survey of Armed Conflicts, Self-Determination Movements, and Democracy," Report. College Park, MD: Center for International Development and Conflict Management, 2000; Carnegie Commission on Preventing Deadly Conflict. "Preventing Deadly Conflict," Report. New York: Carnegie Corporation of New York, 1997; Gurr, TR. "The Challenge of Resolving Ethnonational Conflicts," in: *Peoples Versus States: Minorities at Risk in the New Century* (Gurr, TR, ed), 195–211. Washington, DC: United States Institute of Peace, 2000.

11 The term *state* (or *nation-state*) refers to legal entities with defined populations and territories that are the main actors in international relations. The commonly used term *nations* is less precise, often referring to groups with common ethnic identities, while *country* generally refers to a geographical rather than a political entity. This report primarily uses *state* but occasionally refers to states as *countries* where the meaning is clear.

12 Cilluffo FJ. "The Threat Posed from the Convergence of Organized Crime, Drug Trafficking, and Terrorism," Testimony, U.S. House Committee on the Judiciary, Subcommittee on Crime. Washington, DC, Nov 13, 2001; Smillie I, Gberie L, Hazleton R. *The Heart of the Matter: Sierra Leone, Diamonds and Human Security*. Ottawa, Partnership Africa Canada, 2000; Friedman TL. *Longitudes and Attitudes: Exploring the World After September 11*. New York: Farrar Straus & Giroux, 2002.

13 Crocker CA. Engaging Failed States. *Foreign Affairs* 82(5): 32–44 (2003).

14 Wallensteen P, Sollenberg M. Armed Conflict, 1989–2000. *Journal of Peace Research* 38(5):629–644 (2001). IRIN. "Key Challenges on Civilian Protection in Conflict," News Brief. Nairobi: UN Office for the Coordination of Humanitarian Affairs, April 3, 2003.

15 Esty DC and others. State Failure Task Force Report: Phase II Findings. *Environmental Change & Security Report* 5: 49–72 (1999); Collier P, Hoeffler A. Greed and Grievance in Civil War. Washington, DC: World Bank, 2001; Collier P. *Breaking the Conflict Trap: Civil War and Development Policy*. Washington, DC: World Bank, Oxford Univ. Press, 2003.

16 Esty DC and others. State Failure Task Force Report: Phase II Findings. *Environmental Change & Security Report* 5: 49–72 (1999).

17 Moller H. Youth as a Force in the Modern World. *Comparative Studies in Society and History* 10: 237–260 (1967/68).

18 Mesquida CG, Wiener NI. Human Collective Aggression: A Behavioral Ecology Perspective. *Ethology and Sociobiology* 17: 247–262 (1996); Ñ. Male Age Composition and the Severity of Conflicts. *Politics in the Life Sciences* 18(2): 181–189 (1999); Ñ. "Age Composition of the Male Population in the Genesis of Violent Conflicts," Paper presented at The Annual Conference of the Population Association of America, Washington, DC, March 30, 2001.

19 According to the UN in 2003, about 3.36 billion people were projected to be living in countries with total fertility rates of less than 2.5 children per woman; see UN Population Division. *World Population Prospects: The 2002 Revision*, POP/DB/WPP/Rev.2002. New York: UN, 2003.

20 Livi-Bacci M. *A Concise History of World Population*. Cambridge, MA: Blackwell, 1992.

21 Lutz W, O'Neill BC, Scherbov S. Europe's Population at a Turning Point. *Science* 299: 1991–1992 (2003); Demeny, P. Population Policy Dilemmas in Europe at the Dawn of the Twenty-first Century. *Population and Development Review* 29(1): 1–28.

22 Smith L, Haddad L. "Overcoming Child Malnutrition in Developing Countries: Past Achievements & Future Choices," Report 30. International Food Policy Research Institute, Washington, DC: IFPRI, 2000; Lutz W, Goujon A. The World's Changing Human Capital Stock: Multi-state Population Forecasts by Educational Attainment. *Population and Development Review* 27(2):323–339 (2001); Bongaarts J, Mauldin WP, Phillips JF. The Demographic Impact of Family Planning Programs. *Studies in Family Planning* 21(6): 299–310 (1990).

23 Montgomery MR, Cohen B (eds). *From Death to Birth: Mortality Decline and Reproductive Change*. Washington, DC: National Academy Press, 1998.

24 For this estimate, early-transition countries were assumed to have total fertility rates of 4.5 children per woman or more (for 2000–2005, a total of 47

countries, each with a population over 150,000), and middle-transition countries 3.5 to 4.5 children per woman (22 countries). These 69 countries comprised nearly 1 billion people. The northern states of India, averaging more than 3.5 children per woman, add another 500 million people.

25 DaVanzo J, Grammich C. "Dire Demographics: Population Trends in the Russian Federation," MR-1273-WFHF/DLPF/RF. Santa Monica: RAND, 2001; Feshbeck M, Friendly A. Ecocide in the USSR: Health and Nature Under Siege. New York: Basic Books, 1992.

26 Carnegie Commission on Preventing Deadly Conflict. *Preventing Deadly Conflict.* New York: Carnegie Corporation of New York, 1997.

27 Wallensteen P, Sollenberg M. Armed Conflict, 1989–2000. *Journal of Peace Research* 38(5):629–644 (2001); Gleditsch NP, Wallensteen P, Eriksson M, Sollenberg M, Strand H. Armed Conflict 1946–2001: A New Dataset. *Journal of Peace Research* 39(5):615–637 (2002).

28 Collier P, Hoeffler A, Söderbom M. "On the Duration of Civil War," Discussion Paper. Washington, DC: World Bank, Development Research Group, 2001; Gurr TR, Marshall MG, Khosla D. *Peace and Conflict 2001: A Global Survey of Armed Conflicts, Self-Determination Movements, and Democracy.* College Park, MD: Center for International Development and Conflict Management, 2000.

29 Trends in population-wide death rates proved less useful than birth rates or infant mortality rates in discerning patterns of risk along the demographic transition. This may reflect at least in part the fact that death rates decline in the early parts of the transition as childhood diseases are overcome, but tend to rise again, modestly, as median age increases and old-age mortality becomes more common.

30 Historical evidence reviewed in: Livi-Bacci M. *A Concise History of World Population.* Cambridge, MA: Blackwell, 1992.

31 UN Population Division. *World Population Prospects: The 2002 Revision*, 2003.

32 Lutz W, O'Neill BC, Scherbov S. Europe's Population at a Turning Point. *Science* 299: 1991–1992 (2003); Demeny, P. Population Policy Dilemmas in Europe at the Dawn of the Twenty-first Century. *Population and Development Review* 29(1): 1–28 (2003).

33 Chua AL. *World On Fire: How Exporting Free Market Democracy Breeds Ethnic Hatred and Global Instability.* New York: Doubleday, 2002.

34 Karatnycky A (ed). *Freedom in the World: The Annual Survey of Political Rights and Civil Liberties, 2001–2002.* New York: Freedom House, 2002.

35 Mansfield, ED, Snyder J. Democratization and the Danger of War. *International Security* 20(1): 5–38 (1995), (note: data from Polity II data set and Correlates of War data); Esty DC and others. State Failure Task Force Report: Phase II Findings. *Environmental Change & Security Report* 5: 49–72 (1999), (note: data from Polity II data set); Gurr TR, Marshall MG, Khosla D. *Peace and Conflict 2001: A Global Survey of Armed Conflicts, Self-Determination Movements, and Democracy.* College Park: Center for International Development and Conflict Management, Univ. of Maryland, 2000.

36 East West Center. *The Future of Population in Asia.* Honolulu: EWC, 2002.

37 East-West Center. "The Future of Population in Asia," Report. Honolulu: EWC, 2002; Bloom DE, Canning D, Sevilla J. "The Demographic Dividend: A New Perspective on the Economic Consequences of Population Change," MR-1274-WFHF/DLPF/RF/UNPF, Santa Monica: RAND, 2002; World Bank. *The East Asian Miracle: Economic Growth and Public Policy.* London: Oxford Univ. Press, 1993; Asian Development Bank. 1997. *Emerging Asia: Changes and Challenges.* Manila: ADB; Mason A (ed). *Population Change and Economic Development in East Asia: Challenges Met, Opportunities Seized.* Stanford: Stanford Univ. Press, 2001; Birdsall N, Kelley AC, Sinding SW (eds). *Population Matters: Demographic Change, Economic Growth and Poverty in the Developing World.* London: Oxford Univ. Press, 2001; Cincotta RP, Engelman R. "Economics and Rapid Change: the Role of Population Growth," Occ. Paper 3. Washington, DC: Population Action International, 1997.

38 Bauer JG. Demographic Change, Development, and the Economic Status of Women in East Asia, in: *Population Change and Economic Development in East Asia: Challenges Met, Opportunities Seized* (Mason A, ed), p. 359–384. Stanford: Stanford University Press.

39 Williamson JG. Demographic Change, Economic Growth, and Inequality, in: *Population Matters: Demographic Change, Economic Growth, and Poverty*

in the Developing World (Birdsall N, Kelley AC, Sinding SW, eds), p 107–136. Oxford: Oxford Univ. Press, 2001; Williamson JG, Higgins M. "The Accumulation and Demography Connection in East Asia, in: *Proceedings of the Conference on Population and the East Asian Miracle).* Honolulu: East-West Center, 1997.

40 Laipson E. The Middle East's Demographic Transition: What Does It Mean? *Journal of International Affairs* 56(1): 175–188 (2002); Cincotta RP. Global Trends 2015- A Demographic Perspective. *Environmental Change and Security Project Report* 7: 64–66 (2001).

41 Ogawa N, Retherford RD. Shifting costs of caring for the elderly back to families in Japan: will it work? *Population and Development Review* 23(1): 59–94 (1997).

42 Bauer JG. "How Japan and the Newly Industrialized Economies of Asia are Responding to Labor Scarcity," Asia-Pacific Research Report 3. Honolulu: East-West Center, 1995.

43 Grammich C. "Conflict and Population Trends in Religion," Paper presented at the Population Association of America Meeting, Atlanta, GA, May 9, 2002 (Although the author's conclusions are preliminary in this paper, he finds some evidence that a group's relative decline in "population share" is associated with the initiation of conflict); Fox J. Towards a Dynamic Theory of Ethno-Religious Conflict. *Nations and Nationalism* 5(4): 431–463 (1999).

44 For a review of the activities of the Somali warlord Mohammed Farah Aidid, see: Bacevich AJ. Learning from Aidid. *Commentary* 96(6):30–33 (1993). Descriptions of Slobodan Milosevic's involvement in Bosnia's civil conflict can be obtained from the proceedings of the International Criminal Tribunal for the Former Yugoslavia, accessed at: www.un.org/icty (last accessed September 1, 2003). Jean Kambanda's ascent to power and complicity in atrocities in Rwanda are described in the proceedings of the International Criminal Tribunal for Rwanda, accessed at www.ictr.org (last accessed September 1, 2003).

45 Fearon JD, Laitin DD. Ethnicity, Insurgency, and Civil War. *American Political Science Review* 97(1): 75–90 (2003).

46 International relations literature on ethnic relations and the state comes from several perspectives. For examples of what political scientists refer to as the primordialist approach, see: Vanhanen, T. *Ethnic Conflicts Explained by Ethnic Nepotism.* Stamford, CT: JAI Press, 1999; Vanhanen, T. "Domestic Ethnic Conflict and Ethnic Nepotism: A Comparative Analysis." *Journal of Peace Research* 36(1): 55–73 (1999); Easterly W, Levine R. "Africa's Growth Tragedy: Policies and Ethnic Divisions." *Quarterly Journal of Economics* 112(4):1203–1250 (1997); For examples of the instrumentalist approach, see: Lake DA, Rothchild D. "Spreading Fear: The Genesis of Transnational Ethnic Conflict," in *The International Spread of Ethnic Conflict: Fear, Diffusion, and Escalation,* (Lake DA, Rothchild D, eds), pp 3–32. Princeton: Princeton Univ. Press, 1999 (see pp 5–7); And the constructivist approach is described in: Gurr TR. *Peoples Versus States: Minorities at Risk in the New Century.* Washington, DC: Institute of Peace Press, 2000.

47 Conly SR, de Silva S. *Paying Their Fair Share? Donor Countries and International Population Assistance.* Washington, DC: Population Action International, 1998.

48 Cross H, Hardee K, Ross J. "Completing the Demographic Transition in Developing Countries," Policy Occ. Paper 8. Washington, DC: The Futures Group, 2002.

49 AbouZahr C, Wardlaw T. U.N. Warns of Increasing Maternal Deaths in Developing Countries. *Bulletin of the World Health Organization* 79: 561–568 (2001).

50 Global population projections from: United Nations (UN). *World Population Prospects: The 2002 Revision.* New York: United Nations, Department for Economic and Social Information and Policy Analysis, Population Division, 2003; UN Population Division. *World Population Prospects: 1990.* New York: United Nations, 1991.

51 Alan Guttmacher Institute. *Sharing Responsibility: Women, Society and Abortion Worldwide.* New York: AGI, 1999; Daulaire N, and others. *Promises to Keep: The Toll of Unintended Pregnancies on Women's Lives in the Developing World.* Washington, DC: Global Health Council, 2002.

52 UN Population Division. *World Population Prospects: The 2002 Revision,* POP/DB/WPP/Rev.2002/ 4/F2. New York: United Nations, Dept. of Economic and Social Affairs, 2003.

53 Fuller G. The Demographic Backdrop to Ethnic Conflict: A Geographic Overview, in: *The Challenge of Ethnic Conflict to National and International Order*

in the 1990s: Geographic Perspectives, p 151– 154. Washington, DC: Central Intelligence Agency, 1995; Fuller G, Pitts FR. Youth Cohorts and Political Unrest in South Korea. *Political Geography Quarterly* 9(1): 9–22 (1990); Huntington SP. *The Clash of Civilizations*. Carmichael, CA: Touchstone Books, 1998.

54 Barker G. "What About Boys?" WHO/FCH/CAH/00.7. Geneva: Dept. of Child and Adolescent Health and Development, World Health Organization, 2000, p 15–16.

55 Simon RJ, Baxter S. Gender and Violent Crime, in: *Violent Crime, Violent Criminals* (Wolfgang ME, Weiner NA, eds). London: Sage, 1989; Daly M, Wilson M. *Homicide*. New York: Aldine de Gruyter, 1988.

56 Archer J. Violence Between Men, in: *Male Violence* (Archer J, ed), p 121–140. New York: Routledge, 1994.

57 Moller H. Youth as a Force in the Modern World. *Comparative Studies in Society and History* 10: 237–260 (1967/68).

58 Goldstone JA. *Revolution and Rebellion in the Early Modern World*. Berkeley: Univ. of California Press, 1991.

59 Mesquida CG, Wiener NI. Human Collective Aggression: a Behavioral Ecology Perspective. *Ethology and Sociobiology* 17: 247–262 (1996); Mesquida CG, Wiener NI. Male Age Composition and the Severity of Conflicts. *Politics in the Life Sciences* 18(2): 181–189 (1999).

60 Urdal H. "Population Pressure and Domestic Conflict: Assessing the Role of 'Youth Bulges' in the Onset of Conflict, 1950–2000," Paper presented at the Fourth Pan-European International Relations Conference, Univ. of Kent, Canterbury, UK, Sept. 9, 2001; Cincotta RP "Are Proportions of Young Males and Measures of Institutional Capacity Meaningful Predictors of Vulnerability to Intra-State Conflict?" Paper presented at the Annual Meeting of the Population Association of America, Atlanta, GA, USA, May 9, 2002.

61 Fuller G, Pitts FR. Youth Cohorts and Political Unrest in South Korea. *Political Geography Quarterly* 9(1): 9–22 (1990); Fuller G. The Demographic Backdrop to Ethnic Conflict: A Geographic Overview, in: *The Challenge of Ethnic Conflict to National and International Order in the 1990s: Geographic Perspectives*. p 151–154. Washington, DC: Central Intelligence Agency, 1995.

62 Caprioli M. Gendered Conflict. *Journal of Peace Research* 37(1): 55–68 (2000); Fite D, Genest M, Wilcox C. Gender Differences in Foreign Policy Attitudes. *American Political Science Quarterly* 18: 492–513 (1990); de Boer C. The Polls: The European Peace Movement and Deployment of Nuclear Missiles. *Public Opinion Quarterly* 49: 119–132 (1985); Hudson V, A Den Boer. A Surplus of Men, A Deficit of Peace. *International Security* 26(4): 5–38 (2002).

63 United Nations Economic and Social Council. "World Youth Report 2003," E/CN.5/2003/4. New York: UN, 2003.

64 Hope KR. Urbanization and Urban Growth in Africa. *Journal of Asian and African Studies* 33(3): 345–358 (1998).

65 UN Population Division. "World Urbanization Prospects: The 2001 Revision, Data Tables and Highlights," ESA/P/WP.173. New York: United Nations, 2002.

66 National Intelligence Council. "Global Trends 2015: A Dialogue About the Future With Nongovernment Experts," NIC 2000–02. Washington, DC: National Foreign Intelligence Board, 2000; Nichiporuk B. "The Security Dynamics of Demographic Factors," MR-1088-WFHF/RF/DLPF/A. Santa Monica: RAND, 2000.

67 Brennan-Galvin E. Crime and Violence in an Urbanizing World. *Journal of International Affairs* 56(1): 123–145 (2002).

68 Brockerhoff M. Migration and the Fertility Transition in African Cities, in: *Migration, Urbanization, and Development: New Directions and Issues* (Bilsborrow RE, ed). Norwell, MA: Kluwer Academic Publishers, 1996.

69 Fuller G, FR Pitts. Youth Cohorts and Political Unrest in South Korea. *Political Geography Quarterly* 9(1): 9–22 (1990).

70 Gizewski P, Homer-Dixon T. "Urban Growth and Violence: Will the Future Resemble the Past?" Project on Environment, Population and Security. Washington, DC: American Association for the Advancement of Sciences, 1995; Renner M. Environmental and Social Stress Factors, Governance, and Small Arms Availability: The Potential for Conflict in Urban Areas, in: *Urbanization, Population, Environment and Security* (Rosan C, Ruble BA, Tulchin JS, eds), p 51–72. Washington, DC: Woodrow Wilson International Center for Scholars, 2000.

71 Chengappa R, Menon R, "The New Battlefields," *India Today*, Jan 31, 1993, p 28; Gizewski P, Homer-Dixon T. "Urban Growth and Violence: Will the Future Resemble the Past?" Project on Environment, Population and Security. Washington, DC: American Association for the Advancement of Sciences, 1995.

72 Human Rights Watch. "We Have No Orders to Save You: State Participation and Complicity in Communal Violence in Gujarat," Vol. 4, no. 3C. New York: HRW, 2002.

73 UN Population Division. "World Urbanization Prospects: The 2001 Revision, Data Tables and Highlights," ESA/P/WP.173. New York: United Nations, 2002.

74 Hope KR. Urbanization and Urban Growth in Africa. *Journal of Asian and African Studies* 33(3): 345–358 (1998).

75 Randall S. The Consequences of Drought for the Populations in the Malian Gourma, in: *Population and Environment in Arid Regions* (Clarke JI, Noin D, eds), p 149–175. Paris: UNESCO, Parthenon, 1998; Rakodi C. Global Forces, Urban Change, and Urban Management in Africa, in: *The Urban Challenge in Africa: Growth and Management of its Large Cities* (Rakodi C, ed). New York: United Nations University Press, 1997.

76 Brockerhoff M, Brennan E. The Poverty of Cities in the Developing World. *Population and Development Review* 24(1): 75–114 (1998).

77 Glenn RW. *Marching Under Darkening Skies: The American Military and the Impending Urban Operations Threat*. Santa Monica: RAND, 1998; Faurby I, Magnusson M-L. The Battle(s) of Grozny. *Baltic Defence Review* 2: 75–87 (1999); Bacevich AJ. Learning from Aidid. *Commentary* 96(6): 30–33 (1993).

78 UN Population Division. "World Urbanization Prospects: The 2001 Revision, Data Tables and Highlights," ESA/P/WP.173. New York: United Nations, 2002.

79 Singapore receives about half of its fresh water from Malaysia via pipeline. The United States pipes a portion of Mexico's allocated Colorado River Waters from San Diego to Tijuana and Baja California. Also, since 1998 Turkey has sent several cubic kilometers of fresh water each year to the Turkish enclave in Cyprus and its 30,000 troops deployed there. A Turkish vessel hauls the river water 100 kilometers across the Mediterranean Sea in immense plastic bladders, carrying about 10,000 cubic meters of fresh water in each. See: Theodoulou M..On Dry, Divided Island of Cyprus, 'Just Add Water' Only Raises Heat. *Christian Science Monitor*, p. 6, July 31,1998.

80 Ohlsson L. "Livelihood Conflicts- Linking Poverty and Environment as Causes of Conflict," Report. Stockholm: SIDA, Environmental Policy Unit, 2000.

81 Homer-Dixon TF. *The Environment, Scarcity and Violence*. Princeton: Princeton Univ. Press, 1999; Lowi MR. Water and Conflict in the Middle East and South Asia: Are Environmental issues and Security Issues Linked? *Journal of Environment and Development* 8(4): 376–396 (1999).

82 Postel S, Wolf AT. Dehydrating Conflict. *Foreign Policy* (Sept/Oct): 60–67 (2001). Conca K, Dabelko GD. Problems and Possibilities of Environmental Peacemaking, in *Environmental Peacemaking* (Conca K, Dabelko GD, eds), p 220–233. Washington, DC: Woodrow Wilson International Center for Scholars, 2002.

83 Rosegrant MW, Cai X, Cline SA. *World Water and Food to 2025: Dealing with Scarcity*. Washington, DC: International Food Policy Research Institute, 2002.

84 Postel S, Wolf AT. Dehydrating Conflict. *Foreign Policy* (Sept/Oct):60–67 (2001).

85 Turner FJ. *The Frontier in American History*. New York: Henry Holt and Company, 1935.

86 Nations JD. The Ecology of the Zapatista Revolt. *Cultural Survival Quarterly* 18(1): 31–33 (1994); Howard P, Homer-Dixon T. "Environmental Scarcity and Violent Conflict: the Case of Chiapas, Mexico," Case Study, Project on Environment, Population and Security (PEPS). Washington, DC: American Association for the Advancement of Science (AAAS), 1995.

87 Lowi MR. Water and Conflict in the Middle East and South Asia: Are Environmental Issues and Security Issues Linked? *Journal of Environment and Development* 8(4): 376–396 (1999); Homer-Dixon, TF. *The Environment, Scarcity and Violence*. Princeton: Princeton University Press, 1999; Kelly K, Homer-Dixon T. "Environmental Scarcity and Violent Conflict: The Case of Gaza," Case Study, PEPS. Washington, DC: AAAS, 1996.

88 Kahl CH. Population Growth, Environmental Degradation, and State-Sponsored Violence: the Case of Kenya, 1991–93. *International Security* 23(2): 80–119 (1999).

89 International Crisis Group. "The Politics of National Liberation and International Division," ICG Africa Report 52. Brussels: ICG, 2002.

90 The origins of these benchmarks are explored more fully in: Engelman R, LeRoy P. *Sustaining Water: Population and the Future of Renewable Water Supplies,* Washington, DC: Population Action International (PAI),1993; Engelman R, LeRoy P. *Conserving Land: Population and Sustainable Food Production,* Washington, DC: PAI, 1995.

91 UN Population Division. *World Population Prospects: The 2002 Revision,* Data, POP/DB/WPP/Rev.2002/1/F8. New York: United Nations, 2003.

92 Greener R. "AIDS and Macroeconomic Impact," in: *State of the Art: AIDS and Economics* (Forsythe S, ed). Washington, DC: International AIDS-Economics Network, 2002, p 49–54.

93 Loewenson R, Whiteside A. "Social and Economic Issues of HIV/AIDS in Southern Africa," Consultancy report. Harare: SAfAIDS, 1997.

94 Husain I, Badcock-Walters P. "Economics of HIV/AIDS Impact Mitigation: Responding to Problems of Systemic Dysfunction and Sectoral Capacity," in: *State of the Art: AIDS and Economics*, (Forsythe S, ed), p 49–54. Washington, DC: International AIDS-Economics Network, 2002.

95 UN Population Division. *World Population Prospects: The 2002 Revision (Highlights),* ESA/P/WP. 180. New York: United Nations, 2003.

96 United Nations Joint Programme on HIV/AIDS (UN-AIDS). Report on the Global HIV/AIDS Epidemic," Geneva: UNAIDS; Greener R. "AIDS and Macroeconomic Impact," in: *State of the Art: AIDS and Economics* (Forsythe S, ed), p 49–54. Washington, DC: International AIDS-Economics Network, 2002.

97 UNAIDS. "Report on the Global HIV/AIDS Epidemic," UNAIDS/02.26E. Geneva: UNAIDS, 2002, p 206.

98 Loewenson R, Whiteside A. "HIV/AIDS: Implications for Poverty Reduction," Background Paper. Geneva: UNDP & UNAIDS, 2001.

99 Agyarko RD and others. "Impact of AIDS on Older People in Africa: Zimbabwe Case Study," WHO/NMH/NPH/ALC/02.12. Geneva: World Health Organization, 2002.

100 UNAIDS. Report on the Global HIV/AIDS Epidemic. UNAIDS/02.26E. Geneva: UNAIDS, 2002, p. 134.

101 Cutcher C. "Survival at the Periphery of Underdevelopment: Street Children in Nairobi, Kenya," Paper presented at the Institute for the African Child Inaugural Conference, Ohio University, Athens, OH, June 16–20, 1999.

102 Nampanya-Serpell N. "Social and Economic Risk Factors for HIV/AIDS-Affected Families in Zambia," Conference paper, IAEN AIDS and Economics Symposium, Durban, South Africa, July 7–8, 2000; UN-AIDS. Report on the Global HIV/AIDS Epidemic. Geneva: UNAIDS, July 2002.

103 Sarin R. A New Security Threat: HIV/AIDS in the Military. *World Watch* (March/April):17–22 (2003); Schneider M, Moodie M. "The Destabilizing Impacts of HIV/AIDS," Report. Washington, DC: Center for Strategic and International Studies, 2002.

104 This estimate is based upon Population Action International's evaluation of several sources, including: Butcher T. "HIV and Lack of Funds Paralyse S. Africa's Army," News.telegraph.co.uk, July 16, 2002; Heinecken L. "Strategic Implications of HIV/AIDS in South Africa." *Conflict, Security and Development* 1(1):109–115 (2001); UNAIDS. "AIDS and the Military: UNAIDS Point of View," Geneva: UN Joint Programme on HIV/AIDS, May 1998; International Crisis Group. "HIV/AIDS as a Security Issue," Report. Washington & Brussels: ICG, June 19, 2001; The Namibian. "AIDS: An Intelligence Issue," February 13, 2001; Armed Forces Medical Intelligence Center. "Impact of HIV/AIDS on Military Forces: Sub-Saharan Africa," DI-1817–2–00 (unclassified portions only). Washington, DC: Defense Intelligence Agency, 2000.

105 Mills G. AIDS and the South African Military: Timeworn Cliché or Timebomb? in: *HIV/AIDS: a Threat to the African Renaissance?* (Lange M, ed), p 67–73. Bonn: Konrad Adenauer Foundation, 2000; Schneider M, Moodie M. "The Destabilizing Impacts of HIV/AIDS," Report. Washington, DC: Center for Strategic and International Studies, 2002.

106 Armed Forces Medical Intelligence Center. "Impact of HIV/AIDS on Military Forces: Sub-Saharan Africa," DI-1817–2–00 (unclassified portions only). Washington, DC: Defense Intelligence Agency, 2000.

107 Yeager R, Kingma S. The HIV/AIDS Pandemic: Program Imperatives and Policy Issues in Civil-Military Relations, in: *HIV/AIDS in Developing Country Militaries.* (Dabelko GD, ed) Washington, DC: Woodrow Wilson Center for International Scholars, in press.

108 United States General Accounting Office. "U.N. Peacekeeping: United Nations Faces Challenges in Responding to the Impact of HIV/AIDS on Peacekeeping Operations," GAO-02–194. Washington, DC: GAO, 2001.

109 UN Security Council Resolution 1308 (2000); Holbrook RC. "HIV/AIDS and International Peacekeeping Operations," Statement to the United Nations Security Council by the United States Permanent Representative, New York, United Nations, July 17, 2000.

110 Boonstra H. As Research Accelerates, Focus Intensifies on Options for 'First-Generation' Microbicide. *Guttmacher Report on Public Policy*, 4 (5), 2001.

111 The female condom (a soft, loose-fitting polyurethane sheath) is inserted in the vagina prior to sexual intercourse. The device's effectiveness ratings for reducing the risk of acquiring a sexually transmitted infection and for reducing the risk of pregnancy are similar to that of the male condom. See: Hatcher RA and others. *Contraceptive Technology* (17ᵗʰ Rev. Ed.). New York: Ardent Media, 1998.

112 Chaya N, Amen K-A, Fox M. "Condoms Count: Meeting the Need in the Era of HIV/AIDS," Report. Washington, DC: Population Action International, 2002. Downloaded at: http://www.popact.org/resources/publications/condomscount/index.htm

113 Shelton JD, Johnston B. Condom Gap in Africa: Evidence from Donor Agencies and Key Informants. *British Journal of Medicine* 323: 139 (2001).

114 UN Population Division. "World Population Prospects: The 2002 Revision (Highlights)," ESA/P/WP. 180. New York: United Nations, 2003.

115 Gordon DF. *The Next Wave of HIV/AIDS: Nigeria, Ethiopia, Russia, India, and China*. Washington, DC: National Intelligence Council, 2002.

116 Gebretensae GT. "HIV/AIDS in the Ethiopian Military: Perceptions, Strategies, and Impacts," Synopsis of Working Paper. Washington, DC: Center for Strategic and International Studies, 2003.

117 Yeager R, Hendrix CW, Kingma S. International Military Immunodeficiency Virus/Acquired Immunodeficiency Syndrome Policies and Programs: Strengths and Limitations in Current Practice. *Military Medicine* 165:87–92 (2000).

118 Sanderson WC. "The Demographic Impact of HIV Medication Programs," Paper presented at the Annual Meeting of the Population Association of America, Atlanta, GA, May 9, 2002; Stover J and others. Can We Reverse the HIV/AIDS Pandemic with an Expanded Response? *Lancet* 360:73 77 (2002).

119 United Nations Population Fund. *Donor Support for Contraceptives and Logistics, 2000*. New York: UNFPA, 2001; Chaya N, Amen K-A, Fox M. Condoms Count: Meeting the Need in the Era of HIV/AIDS. Washington, DC: Population Action International, 2002. Downloaded at: http://www.popact.org/resources/publications/condomscount/index.htm

120 UNAIDS. "Statement of Dr. Peter Piot, Exec. Dir. of the Joint United Nations Programme on HIV/AIDS (UNAIDS), on the signing by Pres. Bush of the Global AIDS Act," UN: Geneva, 2003.

121 Schwartlnder B and others. Resource Needs for HIV/AIDS. *Science* 292: 2434–2436 (2001); UNAIDS. "Despite Substantial Increases, AIDS funding is still only half of what will be needed by 2005," Press Release. UN: Geneva, 2003.

122 Matthew RA. Environmental Stress and Human Security in Northern Pakistan. *Environmental Change and Security Project Report* 7: 17–31 (2001); Martine G, Guzman JM. Population, Poverty, and Vulnerability: Mitigating the Effects of Natural Disasters. *Environmental Change and Security Project Report* 8: 45–64 (2002); Repetto R. *The "Second India" Revisited: Population, Poverty, and Environmental Stress Over Two Decades*. Washington, DC: World Resources Institute, 1994.

123 Fuller G, Pitts FR. Youth Cohorts and Political Unrest in South Korea. *Political Geography Quarterly* 9(1): 9–22 (1990); Gizewski P, Homer-Dixon T. "Urban Growth and Violence: Will the Future Resemble the Past?" Case Study, PEPS. Washington, DC: American Association for the Advancement of Sciences, 1995.

124 International Crisis Group. "HIV/AIDS as a Security Issue," ICG Issues Report. Washington & Brussels: ICG, 2001; see age-structure data from: UN Population Division. "World Population Projections: the 2002 Revision," POP/DB/WPP/ Rev.2002/3/F1, UN: New York, 2003.

APPENDIX 1: **GLOSSARY OF KEY TERMS**

ARMED CONFLICT A violently contested incompatibility including the use of armed force. In this report, statistics concerning armed conflict assume that an armed conflict results in at least 25 battle deaths and involves at least one party associated with a state. [For further details, see Appendix 2A.]

BIRTH RATE The number of births in a year per 1,000 people in the population.

DEMOCRACY A set of political systems in which leaders are elected in competitive multi-party and multi-candidate processes in which opposition parties have a legitimate chance of attaining power or participating in power.[1]

DIASPORA Large-scale, long-term residence of members of an ethnic group outside of the country of the group's perceived origin.

FERTILITY (see total fertility rate)

GUERRILLA WARFARE A tactic used by an armed movement to overturn a government for the purpose of political change. In many instances guerrilla warfare consists of small bands of rebel forces that attack superior government forces.[2]

INFANT MORTALITY RATE The number of deaths to children under one year of age per 1,000 live births in a given year.

INSTITUTIONS The rules of law that the state enforces, the property rights and human rights that it agrees to protect, and the formal agreements it upholds and written policies it pursues.

INSURGENCY An armed insurrection or rebellion against an established system of government within a state.

MEDIAN AGE The age where there are just as many people older in the population as there are younger.

DEATH RATE The number of deaths in a year per 1,000 people in the population.

NON-STATE ACTORS / ORGANIZATIONS Organizations and informal groups without legal ties to a state or states.[3]

POPULATION GROWTH RATE The percentage of the present population by which a population increases annually. The rate can be negative, indicating a decline in population.

POPULATION MOMENTUM The tendency of a population to follow past growth trends for several decades, due to the influence of its age structure, despite immediate changes in fertility that could eventually stabilize population or even reverse its direction of change.

REFUGEE A person who, owing to a well-founded fear of being persecuted for reasons of race, religion, nationality, membership of a particular social group, or political opinion, is outside the country of his nationality, and is unable to or, owing to such fear, is unwilling to avail himself of the protection of that country.[4]

REPLACEMENT OR REPLACEMENT-LEVEL FERTILITY The total fertility rate [see definition, next page] at which the population will ultimately stabilize in the absence of migration (into or out of the population). This level is typically just above two children per woman (as low as 2.04 in some cases) in populations with low rates of childhood mortality. *Note: For the purposes of its medium projection —where medium- and high-fertility countries reach replacement level before 2050, and then remain at that level—the UN Population Division assumes future childhood mortality rates that set this total fertility rate at 2.10 children per woman.*

REPRODUCTIVE HEALTH A state of complete physical, mental and social well-being and not merely the absence of disease or infirmity, in all matters relating to the reproductive system and to its functions and processes. This definition implies that men and women have the right to be informed and to have access to safe, effective, affordable and acceptable methods of family planning of their choice, as well as other methods of their choice for regulation of fertility that are not against the law, and the right of access to appropriate healthcare services that will enable women to go safely through pregnancy and childbirth and provide couples with the best chance of having a healthy infant, and of keeping themselves and their family free of sexually transmitted infections.[5]

REVOLUTION A sudden change in government by collective choice, not brought about through legitimate institutionalized channels such as election, national succession or retirement.[2]

STATE OR NATION-STATE The main actor in international relations, and main agent in international law. It has a permanent population, a defined territory and a government capable of maintaining control over its territory and of conducting international relations with other states.[6]

STATE CAPACITY A state's ability to use the institutions and organizations that it sanctions to respond to change.

STATE FAILURE The outbreak of revolutionary or ethnic wars, abrupt non-electoral changes in the state's ruling regime, or mass killings.[7]

TERRORISM The premeditated use, or threat of use, of extra-normal violence or brutality to gain a political objective through intimidation or fear. Terrorists frequently direct their violence and threats at a large target group or audience, not immediately involved in the political decision-making process that they seek to influence.[2]

TOTAL FERTILITY RATE (TFR) The number of live births that a woman entering her reproductive years would experience, on average, during her lifetime, if the rates of childbearing for women of all ages remained the same during her reproductive years. TFR is a composite indicator, calculated in a population by adding the age-specific fertility rates of women across the span of reproductive years.

SUPPORT RATIO The ratio of working-age adults (ages 15 to 64 years, in the most economically productive years of their lives) to dependents (those aged 14 years and younger and those aged 65 years and older). Populations with high support ratios are endowed with more potential support-providers per dependent than those with low support ratios. *Dependency ratio*, a measure used to convey the same information, is the inverse of the support ratio.

[1] Freedom House. Democracy's Century: A Survey of Global Political Change in the 20th Century," Report. Washington, DC: F.H., 1999.

[2] Sandler T, Hartley K. *The Economics of Defense*. Cambridge: Cambridge Univ. Press, 1995.

[3] Evans G, Newnham J (eds). *Penguin Dictionary of International Relations*. London: Penguin Books, 1998.

[4] UN High Commissioner for Refugees. "The 1951 Convention Relating to the Status of Refugees," Resolution 2198 (XXI) Adopted by the UN General Assembly, July 28, 1951. New York: United Nations, Article 1, p 16.

[5] United Nations Population Fund. *Programme of Action Adopted at the International Conference on Population and Development, Cairo, 5–13 September 1994*. New York: UNFPA, 1996. (The definition is shortened from the World Health Organization definition that appears in this document.)

[6] Convention on Rights and Duties of States (Inter-American). Montevideo, Uruguay, Dec. 26, 1933.

[7] State Failure Task Force. "Final Report of the State Failure Task Force." Washington, DC: Science Applications International Corp. & U.S. Agency for International Development, 1995.

APPENDIX 2: DATA SOURCES AND METHODOLOGIES

A. ARMED CONFLICT DATA Data on armed conflicts are drawn from the *Uppsala Conflict Data Project: States in Armed Conflict*, Uppsala University, Uppsala, Sweden (available online: http://www.pcr.uu.se/research/data.htm).[1] Uppsala researchers define armed conflict as a "contested incompatibility which concerns government and/or territory where the use of armed force between two parties, of which at least one is the government of a state, results in at least 25 battle deaths." All the analyses in this report do not distinguish between the intensity of conflicts. Instead, this report is concerned with the initiation of conflict, and particularly civil conflicts (intrastate conflicts, involving a state and a non-state insurgent or between state factions). Although we did not differentiate between these categories, the Data Conflict Project uses the following categories to denote differences in conflict intensity: (category 1: minor armed conflict) at least 25 battle-related deaths per year and fewer than 1,000 battle-related deaths during the course of conflict; (category 2: intermediate armed conflict) at least 25 battle-related deaths per year and an accumulated total of at least 1,000 deaths, but fewer than 1,000 per year; and (category 3: war) at least 1,000 battle-related deaths per year.

B. DECADES OF ANALYSIS The report's analyses of the outbreak of civil conflict, based on a country's position in the demographic transition (presented in Chapter 2), were conducted on data from three distinct decades. The decade of the 1990s was assumed to last from 1990 through 2000; the 1980s spanned from 1980 to 1990; the 1970s spanned from 1970 to 1980. These 11-year periods were used, rather than regular decades, to increase sample size.

C. POSITION IN THE DEMOGRAPHIC TRANSITION To characterize a country's position in the demographic transition as it entered a decade, its population's birth and death rates were drawn from the five-year period (the United Nations Population Division reports birth and death rates only for 5 year periods) preceding the decade of analysis. For example, analyses of the 1990s were based on birth and death rate data, and infant mortality data, from 1985–90. The immediately previous period was used to avoid the possibility that death and

birth rates observed were a product of the conflict conditions, itself. Birth and death rates, which are calculated using the total population as the base population, change more slowly than total fertility rate. Additional observations concerning these trends used the infant mortality rate of the same five-year period from which birth and death rates were drawn.

D. LIST OF STATES States were drawn from the United Nations current list of countries, using all countries with a population over 150,000. These were modified by combining the principal land mass of a state with its disputed or otherwise separately listed territories (such as adding Hong Kong and Macao's populations into China, and combining France with French overseas territories, the Channel Islands with the United Kingdom, etc.). The list was adjusted for prior decades to correct for the emergence or dissolution of states.

While our analyses began by considering the full complement of countries, those used in calculations performed in this report's analyses varied. The sources of variation were: (1) elimination of countries from the analysis if they were experiencing persistent and recurring conflicts (explained in Appendix 2E); (2) the emergence or dissolution of states; and (3) missing data. For the three decadal analyses of the demographic transition's influences on civil conflict in Chapter 2, the calculations were based on: 118 countries for the 1970s; 125 countries for the 1980s; and 144 countries for the 1990s. Variation in numbers of countries assessed occurs among the analyses of the four demographic stress factors (Chapters 3–6) and the final analysis (Chapter 7), as well. These counts are provided in the discussion of each factor.

E. DEFINING AN OUTBREAK OF CIVIL CONFLICT The object of this methodology was to eliminate, from the analysis, persistent and recurring conflicts. Analyses were concerned only with an *outbreak of civil conflict*—defined as a newly initiated civil conflict; one that neither continued from the five-year period directly preceding the decade of analysis, nor recurred from that period after ceasing for one or more years. Thus, in analyses of the 1990s, states were omitted that experienced a civil conflict that had also occurred during the period 1985 through 1989. Two exceptions were permitted: (1) a civil conflict was counted and the country admitted to the analysis if that conflict was a newly initiated conflict, even though persistent and recurring conflicts were active in other parts of the country; and (2) a country was used in the analysis if the civil conflicts that occurred in the five years previous to that decade, did not resume during the decade.

F. THE LIKELIHOOD OF CIVIL CONFLICT The likelihood of civil conflict for any category in an analysis is equal to the sum of conflicts in the category, divided by the sum of eligible states in the category (after eliminating states with persistent or recurring conflicts). This calculation was considered valid only if more than 20 countries fell into a category. Graphs that portray a profile of the likelihood of civil conflict are displayed where sufficient data existed for analysis.

G. DEFINING DEMOGRAPHIC STRESS CATEGORIES
In each analysis of a demographic factor, the range of demographic data—which were tabulated for states with populations over 150,000—was divided into four categories: low, medium, high and extreme demographic stress categories. Where possible, the values delineating the ranges of the high and extreme categories were based on benchmarks drawn from relevant literature, or derived from available evidence or logical assumptions.

H. THE PROPORTION OF YOUNG ADULTS Researchers who have statistically investigated the role of young adults in the outbreak of violent conflict have approached the question from several perspectives, each employing their own distinct hypothesis. And each hypothesis has spawned its own indicator to express the proportion of young adults in the population. As an indicator with which to measure the population's proportion of young adults in this report, researchers at Population Action International use YA, which expresses the proportion size of a country's population between the ages of 15 and 29 years, males and females, relative to the population of adults, aged 15 years and older. This proportion, is calculated as:

$$YA = \frac{N_{(15-29)}}{N_{(15+)}}$$

where N is the population in the age groups specified in its subscript. This indicator is the easiest to envision, but less sensitive to changes in the most politically volatile portion of the population, young adult males, than other calculations that have been used.

The high and extreme stress benchmarks in this analysis were derived from discussions with Christian Mesquida (University of York, Canada), whose work suggests that a YA over 40 percent is an appropriate estimate for the lower bounds of this category. The categories were arranged as follows: where young adults comprised more than 50 percent of adults, countries were assumed to experience *extreme stress;* from 40 percent to just less than 50 percent, countries were assumed to experience *high stress;* from 30 percent to less than 40 percent, *medium stress;* less than 30 percent, *low stress.* Around 19 percent is about the normal lower bound of this indicator. These data are calculated from age composition estimates by the UN Population Division.[2]

NOTE: Other researchers have focused their investigations on what social scientists have determined to be the most volatile populations—young adult males. Some of these researchers have assumed that these males are between the ages 15 and 29 years, while others have used measures with males between 15 and 24 years old. In his review of the role of young men in violent conflict, Mallory (1970) devised an indicator of the male youth bulge,[3] which he called the *young male ratio*, and which is written below as YMR and calculated as:

$$YMR = \frac{M_{(15-29)} \times 100}{M_{(30+)}}$$

where $M_{(15-29)}$ is the population of young males, aged 15 to 29 years, and $M_{(30+)}$, the population of males of ages 30 and over. In a human behavioral approach to state violence and conflict, such as that employed by Mesquida and Weiner,[4] the indicator YMR has theoretical implications. It suggests a struggle for power between young males and older adult males that is reflected in the relative size of the young adult male subpopulation, vis-à-vis the older male subpopulation.

I. URBAN POPULATION GROWTH Urban population growth rates, estimated and projected by the UN Population Division, were used as the indicator of this demographic factor.[5] The benchmark for the high stress category was assumed to be 4 percent, regarded as an excellent rate of economic growth among high-performing industrial countries. With exceptions, industrial country urban growth rates are typically 1 percent or below. Categories were assumed as follows: where urban population growth rate was at 5.0 percent or greater, countries were assumed to experience *extreme stress* conditions; from 4.0 percent to just less than 5.0 percent, *high stress;* from 1.0 percent to less than 4.0 percent, *medium stress;* less than 1.0 percent, *low stress.*

J. CROPLAND AND RENEWABLE FRESHWATER AVAIL-ABILITY Cropland includes land under temporary and permanent crops, temporary meadows, land under market and kitchen gardens and temporarily fallow land, land under crops that need not be replanted after each harvest, such as cocoa, coffee, fruit and nut trees, rubber and vines. This category excludes land under trees grown for wood or timber. This definition of cropland (measured in hectares) is derived from the World Resources Institute, which aggregates data from the Food and Agricultural Organization's FAOSTAT database. Renewable fresh water data (in cubic meters) are the sum of average annual internal renewable water resources and annual river flows.[6] Population estimates and projections, which were employed to calculate per capita data for the world's countries, are from the United Nations Population Division.

Several of the benchmarks used in this analysis are derived by other researchers. The cropland benchmark of 0.07 hectares per person, for extreme stress, was determined from an historical analysis by Vaclav Smil.[7] Our own analysis finds 0.21 hectares per person as a reasonable benchmark for the high stress category, as few industrialized countries are able to remain agriculturally self-sufficient below this point. Vaclav Smil also finds a population density of between 4 to 5 people per hectare (0.20 to 0.25 ha per person) to be an historic constraint to population growth in agricultural societies before the synthesis of ammonia was industrialized.[8] Malin Falkenmark is the source for two benchmarks for freshwater availability: 1,000 cubic meters per person (extreme stress); 1,667 cubic meters per person (high stress).[9]

For cropland, the following stress categories were used: where availability was less than 0.07 hectares per person, countries were assumed to experience *extreme stress* conditions; from 0.07 to just less than 0.21 hectares per person, *high stress*; from 0.21 to just less than 0.35 hectares per person, *medium stress*; 0.35 hectares per person or more, *low stress*. For freshwater availability, the following categories were used: where availability was less than 1,000 cubic meters per person, countries were assumed to experience *extreme stress*; from 1,000 to just less than 1,667 cubic meters per person, *high stress*; from 1,667 to just less than 3,000 cubic meters per person, *medium stress*; 3,000 cubic meters per person or more, *low stress*.

This analysis was different from those in preceding chapters. The categorizations conducted for both cropland and freshwater availability were integrated. After placing all countries in the most limiting category determined among both resources, the likelihood of civil conflict in each category was calculated as the percentage of countries that experienced civil conflict from 1990 to 2000 (excluding countries with persistent or recurring conflict).

K. DEATH AMONG WORKING-AGE ADULTS, AND HIV PREVALENCE Because of the usual 8- to 12-year delay between HIV infection and death (even without medication), and because of missing data and the variability of estimates of HIV prevalence, particularly in the past, we decided against using HIV prevalence as an indicator of AIDS impact. Because our literature review provided strong indications that death among trained individuals and parents could be the most important influence in the future, the demographic variable that we selected as an appropriate indicator of AIDS impact was the proportion of deaths among working-age adults (those aged 15 to 64 years). Data on age-specific deaths (1995 to 2000) and the size of the working age population were obtained from the UN Population Division (estimates for 1990 to 1995 are not currently available).[10] The benchmark level of precisely 7.0 percent for five-year death losses among working-age adults is based on the recognition that this rate is highly unusual—persistent warfare generally pushes the working-age death toll to somewhere between 4 and 6 percent over five years. Countries were assigned to four demographic stress categories, based upon the proportion of deaths that occurred among working-age adults over a five-year period. The following stress categories were used: where the five-year death toll among working-age adults was greater than 10.0 percent of this group, countries were assumed to experience *extreme stress* conditions; from 7.0 percent to just less than 10.0 percent, *high stress*; from 2.0 percent to less than 7.0 percent, *medium stress*; less than 2.0 percent, *low stress*.

So that the reader can see current estimates of HIV prevalence, these data are mapped, along with working-age adult deaths in Chapter 6. HIV prevalence data are from the United Nations Joint Programme on HIV/AIDS (UNAIDS), and the benchmarks that separate our categories on this map are derived from the UNAIDS categorizations.[11] These categories are not directly comparable to this report's demographic stress categories.

L. ANALYSIS USING MULTIPLE DEMOGRAPHIC FACTORS In this phase of the analysis, we overlap the factors using data from analyses of the 1990s to determine if there is a relationship between multiple demographic stress factors and the likelihood of outbreaks of civil conflict. Overlapping these factors produces a list (and map) of the countries that are most frequently in the high and extreme stress categories (what we call the *critical categories*). The demographic factors used in this analysis are the three that, in previous analyses of the 1990s (discussed in the section entitled "Risk Assessment," in Chapters 3 to 6), provided evidence of contributing to the risk of civil conflict. These were: proportions of young adults in 1995 [see Appendix 2H], the rate of urban population growth from 1990 to 1995 [Appendix 2I], and per capita availability of either cropland or fresh water in 1995 [Appendix 2J]. There was insufficient evidence to warrant using the fourth factor—death rates among working-age adults [see Appendix 2K]. The likelihood of civil conflict for the 1990s is calculated as the count of countries that experienced the outbreak of civil conflict divided by the count in the group. (The four groups are: states with zero, one, two or three critical categories.) For our analysis of 2000 to 2010, the same methods were used to identify countries in critical categories—using 2005 data (2000–05 data for urban population growth)—and to identify countries that are in critical categories multiple times.

[1] Gleditsch NP, Wallensteen P, Eriksson M, Sollenberg M, Strand H. Armed Conflict 1946–2001: A New Dataset. *Journal of Peace Research* 39(5):615–637 (2002); Wallensteen P, Sollenberg M. Armed Conflict, 1989–2000. *Journal of Peace Research* 38(5):629–644 (2001); Wallensteen P, Sollenberg M. Armed Conflict and Conflict Complexes, 1989–97. *Journal of Peace Research* 35(5): 621–634 (1998).

[2] United Nations Population Division. "World Population Prospects: The 2002 Revision," POP/DB/WPP/Rev.2002. New York: UN, 2003.

[3] Durham WH. "Resource Competition and Human Aggression, Part I: A Review of Primitive War." *The Quarterly Review of Biology*, 51, Sept. (1976): 385–415.

[4] Mesquida CG, Wiener NI. Human Collective Aggression: a Behavioral Ecology Perspective. *Ethology and Sociobiology* 17: 247–262 (1996); Mesquida CG, Wiener NI. Male Age Composition and the Severity of Conflicts. *Politics in the Life Sciences* 18(2): 181–189 (1999).

[5] United Nations Population Division. "World Urbanization Prospects: The 2001 Revision," POP/DB/WUP/Rev.2001. New York: UN, 2002.

[6] World Resources Institute. *World Resources 2000–2001: People and Ecosystems, the Fraying of Life.* Washington, DC: WRI, 2000.

[7] Smil V. *Global Ecology: Environmental Change and Social Flexibility.* London: Routledge, 1993.

[8] Smil V. Global Population and the Nitrogen Cycle. *Scientific American* (July): 76–81 (1997).

[9] Falkenmark M, Widstrand C. "Population and Water Resources: A Delicate Balance," Population Bulletin. Washington, DC: Population Reference Bureau, 1992. (The oddly precise indicator of high stress results from the reversal of a round fraction that divides 1,000 meters into thirds.)

[10] United Nations Population Division. "World Population Prospects: The 2002 Revision," POP/DB/WPP/Rev.2002. New York: UN, 2003.

[11] United Nations Joint Programme on HIV/AIDS (UNAIDS). Report on the Global HIV/AIDS Epidemic," Geneva: UNAIDS; Greener R. "AIDS and Macroeconomic Impact," in: *State of the Art: AIDS and Economics* (Forsythe S, ed), p 49–54. Washington, DC: International AIDS-Economics Network, 2002

APPENDIX 3: ILLUSTRATION SOURCES AND STATISTICS

Figures and Tables

FIGURE 1.1 THE ANNUAL NUMBER OF CIVIL AND INTERSTATE CONFLICTS, 1946–2001. Data are from the Conflict Data Project, Uppsala University, and described in: Wallensteen P, Sollenberg M. Armed Conflict, 1989–2000. *Journal of Peace Research* 38(5): 629–644 (2001).

FIGURE 2.1 THE RELATIONSHIP BETWEEN WOMEN'S EDUCATION AND FERTILITY, 1995–2000. A similar graph appears in: Lutz W, Goujon A. The World's Changing Human Capital Stock: Multi-state Population Forecasts by Educational Attainment. *Population and Development Review* 27(2): 323–339 (2001). Data are from various *Demographic and Health Surveys*, which are international data collection efforts sponsored by the US Agency for International Development, and surveyed by *Measure DHS+*, Macro International, Inc. and collaborators (http://www.measuredhs.com).

FIGURE 2.2 THE RELATIONSHIP BETWEEN CONTRACEPTIVE USE AND FERTILITY DECLINE. Data for contraceptive use (CU) in 129 countries, 1995–2000, are from various sources compiled in: Chaya N and others. "A World of Difference: Sexual and Reproductive Health Around the World," Wall chart and report. Washington, DC: Population Action International. Data for 1995–2000 total fertility rate (TFR) are from the UN Population Division, *World Population Prospects: the 2002 Revision*. New York: United Nations, 2003. The linear equation that is the best least-squares fit for these data are: TFR = -5.89(100 CU) + 6.27 (r^2=0.68). Also see: Ropey B, Rutstein SO, Morris L. Fertility Decline in Developing Countries. *Scientific American* 269(6): 60–67 (1993). The five states that deviate most substantially from this line, which appear in the lower left corner of the graph, are Albania, Armenia, Azerbaijan, Georgia, and Ukraine—states where women have used abortion as a means of regulating fertility in the absence of well-developed family planning services.

FIGURE 2.3 COUNTRIES WITH OUTBREAKS OF CIVIL CONFLICT, 1990–2000: THEIR POSITIONS ALONG THE PATH OF DEMOGRAPHIC TRANSITION. Data are from the UN Population Division's tables of crude birth rates (CBR) and crude death rates (CDR), 1985–90, in: UN Population Division. *World Population Prospects: the 2002 Revision*, 2003. For this 5 year period, these data can be modeled by the equation: Expected CDR = 0.0245 (CBR^2) - 1.2608(CBR) + 22.45; (r^2 = 0.71). In this exercise, we analyzed data for 144 states, which included the 15 former Soviet states, states that evolved from the breakups of Yugoslavia and Czechoslovakia. Israel and Occupied Palestinian Territories, listed separately by the UN, were combined. Armed-conflict data were obtained from: Wallensteen P, Sollenberg M. Armed Conflict, 1989–2000. *Journal of Peace Research* 38(5):629–644 (2001). Gleditsch NP, Wallensteen P, Eriksson M, Sollenberg M, Strand H. Armed Conflict 1946–2001: A New Dataset. *Journal of Peace Research* 39(5): 615–637 (2002). The portions of these data are featured in Appendix 5.

TABLE 2.1 THE RELATIONSHIP BETWEEN BIRTHS, DEATHS AND THE LIKELIHOOD OF CIVIL CONFLICT, 1990–2000. Data for this analysis were from: UN Population Division. *World Population Prospects: the 2002 Revision*. 2003; Gleditsch NP and others, 2002.

FIGURE 2.4 RELATIONSHIP BETWEEN DEMOGRAPHIC TRANSITION AND THE LIKELIHOOD OF CIVIL CONFLICT, 1970S, '80S AND '90S. Data for this analysis were from: UN Population Division. *World Population Prospects: the 2002 Revision*. 2003; Gleditsch NP and others, 2002.

FIGURE 2.5 THE PROCESS OF DEMOGRAPHIC TRANSITION: AN IDEALIZED MODEL. This graph is an idealized version of the transition; it does not represent any specific country in the past or future. To make this graphic, we began with the birth and death rates of Mauritius, and smoothed out spikes, particularly in the death rates. We also separated the tops of the birth and death rate curves, so that the beginnings of descent are more distinguishable and added a projected future using the country's medium projection.

FIGURE 2.6 EXAMPLES OF POPULATION AGE STRUCTURES AT PROGRESSIVE STAGES OF THE DEMO-GRAPHIC TRANSITION. The common source of these age composition data is: UN Population Division. *World Population Prospects: The 2002 Revision.* 2003.

FIGURE 2.7 THE ASIAN TIGER MODEL OF DEVELOPMENT, FROM 1965–2000. Data are national income per capita (World Bank Atlas Method) from: World Bank, "World Development Indicators," Database. 2002; and estimates of total fertility rates from: UN Population Division. *World Population Prospects: The 2002 Revision.* 2003. Fertility data for each 5 years, 1965 to 2000, was calculated (in order to match the income data) by averaging the five-year total fertility rate (TFR) estimates before and after the calculated year. Thus, the 1990 TFR was derived from averaging the 1985–90 and 1990–95 TFR estimates provided by the UN Population Division.

FIGURE 3.1 AN EXTREMELY LARGE YOUTH BULGE: POPULATION AGE STRUCTURE IN THE OCCUPIED PALESTINIAN TERRITORIES (WEST BANK AND GAZA), 2000. The source of these data is: UN Population Division. *World Population Prospects: The 2002 Revision.* 2003.

FIGURE 3.2 THE YOUTH BULGE AND ITS ASSOCIATION WITH MILITARISM AND POLITICAL INSTABILITY: JAPAN, SOUTH KOREA, THAILAND AND SRI LANKA. Proportions of young adults were calculated from Japanese census data in: Ogawa N. "Japanese Population by Age and Sex, 1920–2000," Data set. Nihon University Population Research Institute, Tokyo (2002). Fertility data were unavailable for the years during World War II (WWII). Before WWII, fertility was estimated from the prior year's female cohorts, from ages 15 to 49. Fertility estimates after WWII are total fertility rate estimates from the UN Population Division. Fertility for those years was derived by averaging the five-year fertility estimates for the five years previous and after the year calculated. All data for South Korea and Thailand are derived from data published by the UN Population Division. Data for Sri Lanka are derived from: Fuller G. The Demographic Backdrop to Ethnic Conflict: A Geographic Overview, in: *The Challenge of Ethnic Conflict to National and International Order in the 1990s: Geographic Perspectives.* p 151–154. Washington, DC: Central Intelligence Agency, 1995. Data in the study used to characterize youth, originally for ages 15–24 years, were adjusted for ages 15–29 using UN population to estimate the 25–29 cohort. Estimates of the size of the subpopulation of children during each year were used to transform youth, as a proportion of total population, to youth as a proportion of all adults.

TABLE 3.1 THE YOUTH BULGE AND ITS ASSOCIATION WITH CIVIL CONFLICT, 1990–2000. The source of the data used in this analysis is: UN Population Division. *World Population Prospects: The 2002 Revision.* 2003; Gleditsch NP and others, 2002. Data are from 145 countries (extreme and high stress categories, 87 countries; medium, 22; low, 36).

TABLE 3.2 TRENDS IN THE YOUTH BULGE, 1975–2005. The data are estimates of population by age from: UN Population Division. *World Population Prospects: The 2002 Revision.* 2003.

FIGURE 4.1 GROWTH IN THE NUMBER OF CITIES IN THE DEVELOPED AND DEVELOPING COUNTRIES, 1950–2000. Data are from: UN Population Division. *World Urbanization Prospects: The 2001 Revision.* POP/DB/WUP/Rev.2001. New York: United Nations, 2002.

FIGURE 4.2 THE RELATIONSHIP BETWEEN URBAN POPULATION GROWTH AND THE RATE OF NATIONAL POPULATION GROWTH, 1995–2000. The regression line in this figure, relating urban population growth (UR) to the national rate of population growth (PR), both measured in percent per year, can be fit: $UR = 1.46(PR) + 0.24$; ($r^2 = 0.76$). If the Y-intercept is forced to zero, the line can be expressed as: $UR = 1.56(PR)$, ($r^2 = 0.75$). The data are from 177 countries, 1995–2000. Liberia and Sierra Leone have been omitted because of unusually high rates of population growth associated with refugee movements, as have states with populations under 150,000. Sources of data: UN Population Division. *World Urbanization Prospects: The 2001 Revision,* 2002. UN Population Division. *World Population Prospects: The 2002 Revision,* 2003.

TABLE 4.1 URBAN POPULATION GROWTH AND ITS ASSOCIATION WITH CIVIL CONFLICT, 1990–2000. The sources of data used in this analysis are: UN Population Division. *World Urbanization Prospects: The 2001 Revision.* New York: United Nations, 2002; Gleditsch NP and others, 2002. The likelihood of conflict was calculated as the proportion of countries in a category that experienced a new outbreak of civil conflict, from 1990 to 2000. Data comprises values from 144 countries, which excludes conflicts that persisted or reemerged from the late 1980s. Data for population growth are for 1990–1995, and comprise 145 countries (extreme and high stress categories, 38 countries; medium, 71; low, 36).

TABLE 5.1 CROPLAND AND FRESHWATER SCARCITY, 1975–2025. Population data from: UN Population Division. World Population Prospects: The 2002 Revision, 2003. Cropland estimates are from: Food and Agricultural Organization of the United Nations (FAO). "FAOSTAT," Online database. Rome: FAO, 2002. Estimates of country renewable freshwater supplies are from: World Resources Institute. *World Resources 2002–2004*. Washington, DC: WRI, 2003 (which also publishes the FAO cropland data). A note: In 1975, two countries were both cropland and freshwater scarce, with a population of 1.5 million. In 2000, three countries had entered these two scarcity classifications simultaneously, with 73 million people among them. The medium projection for 2025 suggests the possibility that there will nine land- and water-scarce countries, with total population of 204 million by that year.

TABLE 5.2 CROPLAND AND FRESHWATER AVAILABILITY AND CIVIL CONFLICT, 1990–2000. The sources of data used in this analysis are from: UN Population Division. *World Population Prospects: The 2002 Revision*. 2003; World Resources Institute. *World Resources, 2002–2004*. Washington, DC: WRI, 2003; FAO. FAOSTAT Database, 2002; Gleditsch NP and others, 2002. In total, 144 countries are listed in this analysis, all over 150,000 population. Cropland data for Djibouti is unreported, and data for fresh water resource supplies are missing Djibouti and for most small islands states, plus Swaziland, Luxembourg, Cyprus, and Cape Verde. For these states, only freshwater availability per capita was used as an indicator in this analysis. Djibouti was dropped from the analysis.

FIGURE 6.1 BOTSWANA'S AGE STRUCTURE IN 2020: WITH AND WITHOUT THE AIDS EPIDEMIC. The graph appears in the report: McDevitt TM, Stanecki KA, Way PO. *World Population Profile: 1998*. Washington, DC: U.S. Census Bureau, 1999.

TABLE 6.1 HIV PREVALENCE IN SELECTED MILITARIES IN SUB-SAHARAN AFRICA. These estimates appear in: Armed Forces Medical Intelligence Center. *Impact of HIV/AIDS on Military Forces: Sub-Saharan Africa*. DI-1817–2–00 (unclassified sections). Washington, DC: Defense Intelligence Agency, 2000.

TABLE 7.1 DEMOGRAPHIC STRESS FACTORS AND THE LIKELIHOOD OF CIVIL CONFLICT, 1990–2000. These data are compiled from analyses in chapters 3 to 6 (see Maps 3, 4, 5 and 6 for data sources), and use the following armed conflict data base for analysis: Gleditsch NP and others. 2002. The table shows 143 countries. Two countries, China (with rapid urban growth and low cropland or freshwater availability) and Portugal (with rapid urban growth only), are not included in the final table (which would have included 145 countries) because there are too few countries in these groupings (one country in each) for a meaningful analysis.

TABLE 7.2 FOR 2000 TO 2010, 25 COUNTRIES ARE ASSESSED WITH VERY HIGH LEVELS OF DEMOGRAPHIC RISK OF CIVIL CONFLICT. Results of an analysis by Population Action International, based upon data analyzed in Chapters 3 to 6 (see Maps 3, 4, 5 and 6 for data sources). Countries are listed in alphabetical order.

Maps

SUMMARY MAP. A DECADE OF RISK, 2000–2010. Data are the product of analyses from Chapters 3 to 6 (see Maps 3, 4, 5 and 6 for data sources).

MAP 1. ARMED CONFLICTS, 1990–2000. The source of data is: Gleditsch NP, Wallensteen P, Eriksson M, Sollenberg M, Strand H. Armed Conflict 1946–2001: A New Dataset. *Journal of Peace Research* 39(5):615–637 (2002).

MAP 2.1 HUMAN FERTILITY, 1970–1975; MAP 2.2 HUMAN FERTILITY, 2000–2005. National data are estimates (1970–75) and projections (medium variant, 2000–05) from: the UN Population Division. *World Population Prospects: The 2002 Revision*. 2003.

MAP 3. YOUNG ADULTS, 2005. Data are projections (medium variant, 2005) from: UN Population Division. *World Population Prospects: The 2002 Revision*. 2003.

MAP 4. URBAN POPULATION GROWTH, 2000-2005. Data are projections (medium variant, 2000–2005) from: UN Population Division. *World Urbanization Prospects: The 2001 Revision.* 2002.

MAP 5.1 CROPLAND AVAILABILITY, 2005. Data are calculations from population projections (medium variant, 2005) from: UN Population Division, *World Population Prospects: The 2002 Revision,* 2003; and estimates of cropland area from: FAO. FAOSTAT Database, 2002. (These data also can be obtained in the database associated with: World Resources Institute. *World Resources: 2002–2004,* 2003).

MAP 5.2 FRESHWATER AVAILABILITY, 2005. Data are calculations from population projections (medium variant, 2005) from: UN Population Division, *World Population Prospects: The 2002 Revision,* 2003; World Resources Institute. *World Resources: 2002–2004,* 2003.

MAP 6.1 WORKING-AGE DEATHS, 2000-2005. Data are calculations from population projections (medium variant, 2005) from: UN Population Division, *World Population Prospects: The 2002 Revision,* 2003.

MAP 6.2 ADULT HIV PREVALENCE, 2001. Data are from: UN Joint Programme on HIV/AIDS, *Report on the Global HIV/AIDS Epidemic.* Geneva: UNAIDS, 2002.

MAP 7. DEMOGRAPHIC STRESS, 2000-2010. Data are the product of analyses from Chapters 3 to 6 (see Maps 3, 4, 5 and 6 for data sources).

APPENDIX 4: **COUNTRY DATA TABLE**

	Population	Total Fertility Rate	Young Adults (15-29) as a Proportion of all Adults (15+)	Urban Population Growth	Natural Renewable Freshwater Resources	Available Renewable Fresh Water per Capita	Cropland	Available Cropland per Capita	Working-Age Adult (15-64) Death Rate	Adult (15-49) HIV Prevalence	Total Population HIV-positive
Date	2005	2000-05	2005	2000-05	2002	2005	2000	2005	2000-05	2001	2001
Unit Measure	thousands of people	children per woman	percent	percent per year	cubic kilometers	cubic meters per person	thousands of hectares	hectares per person	percent dying over 5-year period	percent	people
SOURCES	(a)	(a)	(a)	(b)	(c)	(a,c)	(d)	(a,d)	(a)	(e)	(e)
Afghanistan	25,971	6.8	47.4	5.7	65	2,503	8,054	0.31	5.1	nd	nd
Albania	3,220	2.3	35.3	2.1	42	13,043	699	0.22	1.0	nd	nd
Algeria	32,877	2.8	45.1	2.7	14	426	8,195	0.25	1.5	0.1	13,000
Angola	14,533	7.2	50.7	4.8	184	12,661	3,300	0.23	7.6	5.5	350,000
Argentina	39,311	2.4	34.7	1.4	814	20,707	27,200	0.69	1.7	0.7	130,000
Armenia	3,043	1.2	34.1	0.2	11	3,615	560	0.18	1.6	0.2	2,400
Australia	20,092	1.7	26.0	1.4	492	24,487	50,600	2.52	1.1	0.1	12,000
Austria	8,120	1.3	21.1	0.2	78	9,606	1,470	0.18	1.3	0.2	9,900
Azerbaijan	8,527	2.1	37.0	0.6	30	3,518	1,907	0.22	1.6	<0.1	1,400
Bahamas	321	2.3	36.3	1.6	nd	nd	11	0.03	3.7	3.5	6,200
Bahrain	754	2.7	35.0	2.0	nd	nd	6	0.01	1.1	0.3	<1,000
Bangladesh	152,593	3.5	45.6	4.3	1,211	7,936	8,484	0.06	2.9	<0.1	13,000
Barbados	272	1.5	27.9	1.4	nd	nd	17	0.06	1.0	1.2	nd
Belarus	9,809	1.2	28.2	-0.2	58	5,913	6,257	0.64	3.0	0.3	15,000
Belgium	10,359	1.7	21.7	0.2	18	1,738	837	0.08	1.3	0.2	8,500
Belize	266	3.2	47.0	2.2	19	71,359	89	0.33	1.8	2.0	2,500
Benin	7,103	5.7	51.9	4.5	25	3,520	2,215	0.31	5.1	3.6	120,000
Bhutan	2,392	5.0	47.7	5.9	95	39,719	160	0.07	2.8	<0.1	<100
Bolivia	9,138	3.8	43.9	3.0	623	68,173	2,206	0.24	2.7	0.1	4,600
Bosnia and Herzegovina	4,209	1.3	26.8	2.2	38	9,029	650	0.15	1.7	<0.1	900
Botswana	1,801	3.7	52.4	1.4	14	7,775	373	0.21	14.0	38.8	330,000
Brazil	182,798	2.2	38.5	1.9	8,233	45,039	65,200	0.36	2.6	0.1	610,000
Brunei Darussalam	374	2.5	40.8	2.5	nd	nd	7	0.02	0.8	nd	nd

nd = NO DATA AVAILABLE

DATA SOURCES: (a) UN POPULATION DIVISION, 2003, (b) UN POPULATION DIVISION, 2002, (c) WORLD RESOURCES INSTITUTE, 2003, (d) FOOD AND AGRICULTURAL ORGANIZATION, 2002, (e) UN JOINT PROGRAMME ON HIV/AIDS, 2002.

	Population	Total Fertility Rate	Young Adults (15-29) as a Proportion of all Adults (15+)	Urban Population Growth	Natural Renewable Freshwater Resources	Available Renewable Fresh Water per Capita	Cropland	Available Cropland per Capita	Working-Age Adult (15-64) Death Rate	Adult (15-49) HIV Prevalence	Total Population HIV-positive
Date	2005	2000-05	2005	2000-05	2002	2005	2000	2005	2000-05	2001	2001
Unit Measure	thousands of people	children per woman	percent	percent per year	cubic kilometers	cubic meters per person	thousands of hectares	hectares per person	percent dying over 5-year period	percent	people
Bulgaria	7,763	1.1	25.1	-0.9	21	2,705	4,636	0.6	2.6	<0.1	nd
Burkina Faso	13,798	6.7	55.1	5.1	13	942	3,850	0.28	7.0	6.5	440,000
Burundi	7,319	6.8	55.6	6.4	4	547	1,260	0.17	8.9	8.3	390,000
Cambodia	14,825	4.8	48.2	5.5	476	32,108	3,807	0.26	4.0	2.7	170,000
Cameroon	16,564	4.6	49.9	3.6	286	17,266	7,160	0.43	7.7	11.8	920,000
Canada	31,972	1.5	24.2	1.1	2,902	90,766	45,700	1.43	1.2	0.3	55,000
Cape Verde	482	3.3	50.2	3.9	nd	nd	41	0.09	1.4	nd	nd
Central African Republic	3,962	4.9	50.1	2.8	144	36,347	2,020	0.51	10.5	12.9	250,000
Chad	9,117	6.7	49.9	4.7	43	4,716	3,550	0.39	6.5	3.6	150,000
Chile	16,185	2.4	32.6	1.5	922	56,965	2,297	0.14	1.4	0.3	20,000
China Including Hong Kong and Macau SARs	1,329,927	1.8	30.4	3.2	2,830	2,128	135,557	0.1	1.6	0.1	850,000
Colombia	45,600	2.6	38.6	2.3	2,132	46,754	4,545	0.1	1.8	0.4	140,000
Comoros	812	4.9	50.2	4.6	nd	nd	128	0.16	2.9	nd	nd
Congo, Democratic Republic	56,079	6.7	52.3	4.9	1,283	22,878	7,880	0.14	7.4	4.9	1,300,000
Congo, Republic	3,921	6.3	51.7	4.0	832	212,217	220	0.06	7.1	7.2	110,000
Costa Rica	4,327	2.3	39.3	2.9	112	25,884	505	0.12	1.1	0.6	11,000
Côte d'Ivoire	17,165	4.7	52.3	3.0	81	4,719	7,350	0.43	9.4	9.7	770,000
Croatia	4,405	1.7	23.9	0.8	106	24,063	1,586	0.36	2.1	<0.1	200
Cuba	11,353	1.6	25.2	0.5	38	3,347	4,465	0.39	1.5	<0.1	3,200
Cyprus	813	1.9	29.1	1.2	nd	nd	143	0.18	1.1	0.3	
Czech Republic	10,216	1.2	25.4	0.0	13	1,273	3,318	0.32	1.8	<0.1	500
Denmark	5,386	1.8	20.7	0.2	6	1,114	2,289	0.43	1.7	0.2	3,800
Djibouti	721	5.7	47.3	1.3	nd	nd	nd	nd	6.9	nd	nd
Dominican Republic	8,998	2.7	41.0	2.4	21	2,334	1,596	0.18	2.7	2.5	130,000
East Timor	857	3.8	49.0	4.7	nd	nd	80	0.09	5.8	nd	nd
Ecuador	13,379	2.8	41.7	2.4	432	32,290	3,001	0.22	1.7	0.3	20,000
Egypt	74,878	3.3	44.2	1.8	58	775	3,291	0.04	1.8	<0.1	8,000
El Salvador	6,709	2.9	43.1	3.5	25	3,726	810	0.12	2.0	0.6	24,000
Equatorial Guinea	521	5.9	46.3	4.9	26	49,920	230	0.44	5.4	3.4	5,900
Eritrea	4,456	5.4	51.0	6.3	6	1,346	501	0.11	5.7	2.8	55,000

	Population	Total Fertility Rate	Young Adults (15-29) as a Proportion of all Adults (15+)	Urban Population Growth	Natural Renewable Freshwater Resources	Available Renewable Fresh Water per Capita	Cropland	Available Cropland per Capita	Working-Age Adult (15-64) Death Rate	Adult (15-49) HIV Prevalence	Total Population HIV-positive
Date	2005	2000-05	2005	2000-05	2002	2005	2000	2005	2000-05	2001	2001
Unit Measure	thousands of people	children per woman	percent	percent per year	cubic kilometers	cubic meters per person	thousands of hectares	hectares per person	percent dying over 5-year period	percent	people
Estonia	1,294	1.2	26.8	-1.1	13	10,045	1,134	0.88	2.8	1.0	7,700
Ethiopia	74,189	6.1	50.3	4.6	110	1,483	10,728	0.14	7.1	6.4	2,100,000
Fiji	854	2.9	40.8	2.5	29	33,939	285	0.33	2	0.1	300
Finland	5,224	1.7	22.6	0.1	110	21,058	2,191	0.42	1.5	<0.1	1,200
France	60,711	1.9	23.4	0.6	204	3,360	19,582	0.32	1.3	0.3	100,000
Gabon	1,375	4.0	47.2	3.4	164	119,253	495	0.36	4.7	nd	nd
Gambia	1,499	4.7	44.4	4.4	8	5,336	235	0.16	4.6	1.6	8,400
Georgia	5,026	1.4	28.4	-0.1	63	12,535	1,062	0.21	1.9	<0.1	900
Germany	82,560	1.4	20.3	0.2	154	1,865	12,020	0.15	1.4	0.1	41,000
Ghana	21,833	4.1	49.2	3.1	53	2,428	5,809	0.27	4.2	3.0	360,000
Greece	10,978	1.3	22.5	0.5	74	6,740	3,854	0.35	1.2	0.2	8,800
Guatemala	12,978	4.4	49.7	3.4	111	8,553	1,905	0.15	2.6	1.0	67,000
Guinea	8,788	5.8	49.2	3.1	226	25,717	1,485	0.17	5.1	1.5	52,000
Guinea-Bissau	1,584	7.1	49.1	4.8	31	19,576	350	0.22	5.9	2.8	17,000
Guyana	768	2.3	40.4	1.4	241	313,801	496	0.65	3.0	2.7	18,000
Haiti	8,549	4.0	51.5	3.3	14	1,638	910	0.11	6.9	6.1	250,000
Honduras	7,257	3.7	47.9	4.0	96	13,228	1,427	0.20	2.4	1.6	57,000
Hungary	9,784	1.2	25.2	-0.1	104	10,629	4,803	0.49	2.8	0.1	2,800
Iceland	294	2.0	28.0	0.8	170	578,818	7	0.02	1.0	0.2	220
India	1,096,917	3.0	39.7	2.3	1,897	1,729	169,700	0.15	2.4	0.8	3,970,000
Indonesia	225,313	2.4	39.4	3.6	2,838	12,596	33,546	0.15	2.2	0.1	120,000
Iran, Islamic Republic of	70,675	2.3	49.1	2.4	138	1,953	16,326	0.23	1.4	<0.1	20,000
Iraq	26,555	4.8	47.5	2.7	75	2,824	5,540	0.21	2.6	<0.1	<1000
Ireland	4,040	1.9	31.3	1.4	52	12,871	1,053	0.26	1.2	0.1	2,400
Israel	6,685	2.7	33.2	2.2	2	299	418	0.06	0.8	0.1	2,700
Italy	57,253	1.2	19.3	0.1	191	3,336	10,825	0.19	1.2	0.4	100,000
Jamaica	2,701	2.4	39.9	1.8	9	3,332	274	0.10	1.1	1.2	20,000
Japan	127,914	1.3	20.7	0.4	430	3,362	4,830	0.04	1.1	<0.1	12,000
Jordan	5,750	3.6	46.0	3.0	1	174	401	0.07	1.6	<0.1	<1000
Kazakhstan	15,364	2.0	36.1	-0.3	110	7,159	21,671	1.41	2.7	0.1	6,000
Kenya	32,849	4.0	55.5	4.6	30	913	4,520	0.14	9.3	15.0	2,500,000
Korea, Democratic People's Republic of	22,876	2.0	30.7	1.2	77	3,366	2,000	0.09	3.8	nd	nd
Korea, Republic of	48,182	1.4	28.1	1.3	70	1,453	1,919	0.04	1.5	<0.1	4,000

	Population	Total Fertility Rate	Young Adults (15-29) as a Proportion of all Adults (15+)	Urban Population Growth	Natural Renewable Freshwater Resources	Available Renewable Fresh Water per Capita	Cropland	Available Cropland per Capita	Working-Age Adult (15-64) Death Rate	Adult (15-49) HIV Prevalence	Total Population HIV-positive
Date	2005	2000-05	2005	2000-05	2002	2005	2000	2005	2000-05	2001	2001
Unit Measure	thousands of people	children per woman	percent	percent per year	cubic kilometers	cubic meters per person	thousands of hectares	hectares per person	percent dying over 5-year period	percent	people
Kuwait	2,671	2.7	31.6	2.6	0.02	7	10	0.00	0.7	nd	nd
Kyrgyzstan	5,278	2.6	41.4	1.2	21	3,979	1,435	0.27	2.1	<0.1	500
Lao People's Democratic Republic	5,918	4.8	47.4	4.6	334	56,435	958	0.16	3.8	<0.1	1,400
Latvia	2,265	1.1	26.5	-0.6	35	15,453	1,874	0.83	2.9	0.4	5,000
Lebanon	3,761	2.2	38.0	1.9	4	1,064	332	0.09	1.2	nd	nd
Lesotho	1,797	3.8	53.9	3.4	3	1,669	325	0.18	14.7	31.0	360,000
Liberia	3,603	6.8	52.0	6.8	232	64,394	595	0.17	7.9	nd	nd
Libyan Arab Jamahiriya	5,768	3.0	46.4	2.5	1	173	2,150	0.37	1.4	0.2	7,000
Lithuania	3,401	1.3	26.4	0.0	25	7,350	2,992	0.88	2.5	0.1	1,300
Luxembourg	465	1.7	21.6	1.6	nd	nd	837	0.08	1.3	0.2	nd
Macedonia, TFYR	2,076	1.9	29.9	0.4	6	2,890	599	0.29	1.6	<0.1	nd
Madagascar	18,409	5.7	48.0	4.9	337	18,307	3,500	0.19	4.0	0.3	22,000
Malawi	12,572	6.1	51.2	4.6	17	1,352	2,240	0.18	11.2	15.0	850,000
Malaysia	25,325	2.9	38.8	2.9	580	22,902	7,605	0.3	1.5	0.4	42,000
Maldives	338	5.3	49.9	4.6	nd	nd	3	0.01	1.9	0.1	nd
Mali	13,829	7.0	54.5	5.1	100	7,231	4,674	0.34	5.2	1.7	110,000
Malta	397	1.8	26.8	0.7	nd	nd	9	0.02	1.1	0.1	nd
Mauritania	3,069	5.8	47.4	5.1	11	3,585	500	0.16	4.2	nd	nd
Mauritius	1,244	1.9	33.0	1.6	nd	nd	106	0.09	1.9	0.1	700,000
Mexico	106,385	2.5	41.2	1.7	457	4,296	27,300	0.26	1.6	0.3	150,000
Micronesia, Federated States of	111	3.8	46.8	3.6	nd	nd	36	0.32	1.8	nd	nd
Moldova, Republic of	4,259	1.4	33.4	0.0	12	2,818	2,190	0.51	2.8	0.2	5,500
Mongolia	2,667	2.4	45.3	1.3	35	13,124	1,176	0.44	2.1	<0.1	100
Morocco	31,564	2.7	42.5	2.9	29	919	9,734	0.31	1.6	0.1	13,000
Mozambique	19,495	5.6	49.9	5.1	216	11,080	4,135	0.21	10.2	13.0	1,100,000
Myanmar	50,696	2.9	41.0	2.9	1,046	20,633	10,495	0.21	3.7	nd	nd
Namibia	2,032	4.6	48.7	3.3	18	8,857	820	0.4	10.7	22.5	230,000
Nepal	26,289	4.3	45.5	5.1	210	7,988	2,968	0.11	3.2	0.5	58,000
Netherlands	16,300	1.7	21.5	0.5	91	5,583	944	0.06	1.2	0.2	17,000
New Zealand	3,932	2.0	25.5	0.9	327	83,168	3,280	0.83	1.3	0.1	1,200
Nicaragua	5,727	3.7	49.3	3.3	197	34,396	2,746	0.48	1.9	0.2	5,800

Date	Population	Total Fertility Rate	Young Adults (15-29) as a Proportion of all Adults (15+)	Urban Population Growth	Natural Renewable Freshwater Resources	Available Renewable Fresh Water per Capita	Cropland	Available Cropland per Capita	Working-Age Adult (15-64) Death Rate	Adult (15-49) HIV Prevalence	Total Population HIV-positive
	2005	2000-05	2005	2000-05	2002	2005	2000	2005	2000-05	2001	2001
Unit Measure	thousands of people	children per woman	percent	percent per year	cubic kilometers	cubic meters per person	thousands of hectares	hectares per person	percent dying over 5-year period	percent	people
Niger	12,873	8.0	52.7	6.0	34	2,641	4,500	0.35	5.0	1.4	nd
Nigeria	130,236	5.4	50.2	4.4	286	2,196	30,850	0.24	5.6	5.8	3,500,000
Norway	4,570	1.8	22.5	0.7	382	83,596	883	0.19	1.2	0.1	1,800
Occupied Palestinian Territory	3,815	5.6	48.8	4.1	nd	nd	231	0.06	1.2	nd	nd
Oman	3,020	5.0	44.0	4.0	1	331	80	0.03	1.2	0.1	1,300
Pakistan	161,151	5.1	46.5	3.5	223	1,384	21,960	0.14	2.2	0.1	78,000
Panama	3,235	2.7	37.5	2.0	148	45,755	655	0.20	1.4	1.5	25,000
Papua New Guinea	5,959	4.1	45.7	3.7	801	134,413	855	0.14	4.1	0.7	17,000
Paraguay	6,160	3.8	45.1	3.6	336	54,548	2,378	0.39	1.5	0.1	nd
Peru	27,968	2.9	41.3	2.1	1,913	68,399	4,210	0.15	1.8	0.4	53,000
Philippines	82,809	3.2	44.4	3.2	479	5,784	10,050	0.12	1.7	<0.1	9,400
Poland	38,516	1.3	29.3	0.3	62	1,610	14,330	0.37	2.0	0.1	14,000
Portugal	10,080	1.5	23.9	1.9	69	6,845	2,705	0.27	1.5	0.5	27,000
Qatar	628	3.2	26.7	1.7	nd	nd	21	0.03	1.8	0.1	nd
Romania	22,228	1.3	28.4	0.1	212	9,538	9,865	0.44	2.5	<0.1	6,500
Russian Federation	141,553	1.1	28.3	-0.6	4,313	30,469	126,820	0.90	3.9	0.9	700,000
Rwanda	8,607	5.7	53.5	4.2	5	581	1,150	0.13	9.6	8.9	500,000
Saint Lucia	152	2.3	40.8	1.7	nd	nd	17	0.11	1.7	nd	nd
Saint Vincent and the Grenadines	121	2.2	43.4	2.6	nd	nd	11	0.09	1.1	nd	nd
Samoa	182	4.1	49.3	nd	nd	nd	122	0.67	1.6	nd	nd
Sao Tome and Principe	169	4.0	51.9	3.2	nd	nd	47	0.28	1.6	nd	nd
Saudi Arabia	25,626	4.5	43.6	3.6	2	78	3,785	0.15	1.2	0.1	nd
Senegal	10,587	5.0	50.2	4.0	39	3,684	2,400	0.23	4.6	0.5	27,000
Serbia and Montenegro	10,513	1.7	27.5	0.2	209	19,880	3,736	0.36	2.0	0.2	10,000
Sierra Leone	5,340	6.5	48.3	6.3	160	29,965	550	0.1	9.5	7.0	170,000
Singapore	4,372	1.4	23.4	1.7	nd	nd	1	0.0	1.1	0.2	3,400
Slovakia	5,411	1.3	29.5	0.4	50	9,240	1,576	0.29	2.0	<0.1	nd
Slovenia	1,979	1.1	24.3	-0.1	32	16,168	204	0.10	1.7	<0.1	280
Solomon Islands	504	4.4	49.0	6.0	45	89,214	60	0.12	1.6	nd	nd
Somalia	10,742	7.3	50.8	5.8	14	1,303	1,067	0.10	4.8	1.0	43,000

	Population	Total Fertility Rate	Young Adults (15-29) as a Proportion of all Adults (15+)	Urban Population Growth	Natural Renewable Freshwater Resources	Available Renewable Fresh Water per Capita	Cropland	Available Cropland per Capita	Working-Age Adult (15-64) Death Rate	Adult (15-49) HIV Prevalence	Total Population HIV-positive
Date	2005	2000-05	2005	2000-05	2002	2005	2000	2005	2000-05	2001	2001
Unit Measure	thousands of people	children per woman	percent	percent per year	cubic kilometers	cubic meters per person	thousands of hectares	hectares per person	percent dying over 5-year period	percent	people
South Africa	45,323	2.6	44.2	2.1	50	1,103	15,712	0.35	9.8	20.1	5,000,000
Spain	41,184	1.2	23.3	0.3	112	2,719	18,217	0.44	1.10	0.5	130,000
Sri Lanka	19,366	2.0	34.8	2.4	50	2,582	1,910	0.10	1.5	<0.1	4,800
Sudan	35,040	4.4	45.3	4.7	65	1,855	16,433	0.47	4.1	2.6	450,000
Suriname	442	2.5	41.3	1.3	122	275,799	67	0.15	1.6	1.2	3,700
Swaziland	1,087	4.5	55.8	2.2	nd	nd	190	0.17	15.9	33.4	170,000
Sweden	8,895	1.6	21.6	-0.1	174	19,562	2,706	0.30	1.1	0.1	3,300
Switzerland	7,157	1.4	19.6	nd	54	7,545	437	0.06	1.3	0.5	19,000
Syrian Arab Republic	18,650	3.3	50.5	3.3	26	1,394	5,352	0.29	1.2	0.1	nd
Tajikistan	6,356	3.1	46.2	0.7	16	2,517	860	0.14	1.6	<0.1	200
Tanzania, United Republic of	38,365	5.1	53.1	5.3	91	2,372	4,950	0.13	8.6	7.8	1,500,000
Thailand	64,081	1.9	35.3	2.1	410	6,398	18,000	0.28	2.5	1.8	670,000
Togo	5,129	5.3	50.0	4.2	15	2,925	2,630	0.51	6.3	6.0	150,000
Tonga	106	3.7	44.7	nd	nd	nd	48	0.45	1.9	nd	nd
Trinidad and Tobago	1,311	1.6	37.5	1.0	4	3,051	122	0.09	2.3	2.5	17,000
Tunisia	10,042	2.0	40.8	2.1	5	498	5,014	0.50	1.2	0.1	nd
Turkey	73,302	2.4	39.7	1.9	229	3,124	26,672	0.36	1.4	<0.1	nd
Turkmenistan	5,015	2.7	43.7	2.3	25	4,986	1,695	0.34	1.9	<0.1	nd
Uganda	27,623	7.1	55.2	5.7	66	2,389	6,960	0.25	6.9	5.0	600,000
Ukraine	47,782	1.2	26.9	-0.8	140	2,930	33,496	0.70	3.1	1.0	250,000
United Arab Emirates	3,106	2.8	29.9	2.2	0	0	247	0.08	1.0	0.2	nd
United Kingdom	59,598	1.6	23.2	0.3	147	2,467	5,928	0.10	1.3	0.1	34,000
United States of America	300,038	2.1	26.5	1.2	3051	10,169	179,000	0.60	1.6	0.6	900,000
Uruguay	3,463	2.3	30.0	0.9	139	40,136	1,340	0.39	1.7	0.3	6,300
Uzbekistan	26,868	2.4	44.0	1.4	50	1,861	4,850	0.18	1.7	<0.1	740
Vanuatu	222	4.1	46.7	4.2	nd	nd	120	0.54	1.9	nd	nd
Venezuela	26,640	2.7	40.6	2.1	1,233	46,285	3,400	0.13	1.5	0.5	62,000
Viet Nam	83,585	2.3	42.0	3.1	891	10,660	7,350	0.09	1.9	0.3	130,000
Yemen	21,480	7.0	53.2	5.3	4	186	1,669	0.08	3.0	0.1	9,900
Zambia	11,043	5.6	56.5	2.7	105	9,508	5,279	0.48	15.2	21.5	1,200,000
Zimbabwe	12,963	3.9	58.8	3.7	20	1,543	3,350	0.26	18.1	33.7	2,300,00

Population Action
INTERNATIONAL

Population Action International (PAI) is an independent policy research and advocacy group working to strengthen public awareness and political and financial support worldwide for population programs grounded in individual rights. Founded in 1965, PAI is a private, non-profit group and accepts no government funds. □ At the heart of Population Action International's mission is its commitment to advance universal access to family planning and related health services, and to improve educational and economic opportunities, especially for girls and women. Together, these strategies promise to improve the lives of individual women and their families, while also slowing the world's population growth and helping preserve the environment.